"Truly a master class! With pastoral wisdom and therapeutic skill, Kevin Chapman reminds us that all our emotions are from God and are for our good if used wisely. As a follower of Jesus, I've known and experienced fear, anxiety, anger, and sadness. I just wish I'd had this book years ago! I would've better experienced God's loving presence when flooded with both pleasant and unpleasant emotions. The Bible says to 'not be mastered by anything.' Kevin Chapman shows us that this includes our emotions. But instead of vilifying our emotions, he helps us see that our emotions are a good gift from God and part of how we can love God and others with our mind, body, and soul!"

Jason Cusick, lead pastor at Journey of Faith in Southern California and author of *The Anxiety Field Guide*

"Dr. Kevin Chapman has provided a creative and practical approach to engaging emotions. This truthful integration of Christian faith and cognitive science immerses the whole person in a hopeful experience of exploration, discovery, and renewal. These pages have the feel of a pragmatic Christian workbook, but it is actually a transformational invitation into effective stewardship of head, heart, and body."

Stephen P. Stratton, licensed psychologist and professor of counseling and pastoral care at Asbury Theological Seminary

"I can't say enough about how important it is for every Christ-follower to get out from under the rule of emotional immaturity. Dr. Chapman has laid out a great toolbox here to help us embrace what is useful and let go of what is harmful. I so appreciate his devotion to the Word and pursuit of God's original intent for human emotion."

Matt Reagan, associate pastor of Southeast Christian Church in Louisville, Kentucky

"Kevin Chapman skillfully integrates biblical truth and a transdiagnostic therapy approach to teach readers how to master emotions and overcome neuroticism. While not well understood in the church today, neuroticism inhibits people's joy and undermines their ability to live out their callings. Practical exercises for applying clinical skills and scriptural teaching are woven throughout this manual in a way that will encourage readers in their walk with Christ as they learn the material. Both pastors and counselors will find this resource helpful in working with those they serve."

Ted Witzig Jr., pastor and clinical psychologist

"Faith without works is dead. In *Mastering Our Emotions*, Dr. Chapman creates a spiritual walk that combines the Biblical word with actions leading to emotional healing and wellness."

Angela Neal-Barnett, author of *Soothe Your Nerves: The Black Woman's Guide to Understanding and Overcoming Anxiety, Panic, and Fear*

"Finally! A book that upholds Scripture and science on emotions in an approachable and practical fashion. Dr. Chapman navigates both their purpose and pitfalls. We desperately need this Christian work, which accounts for theology and its whole-person application—mind, body, and spirit. The message is clear: set your mind on Christ with the godly use of emotions rather than being mastered by them."

Justin K. Hughes, licensed professional counselor and owner of Dallas Counseling PLLC

"*Mastering Our Emotions* by Dr. Kevin Chapman is a groundbreaking exploration of the human spirit that offers a refreshing and holistic approach to emotional well-being. Dr. Chapman masterfully combines biblical wisdom and psychological insights, providing an easy-to-follow road map for navigating life's emotional storms. This book is an invaluable resource for anyone seeking to understand and harness the power of their emotions. Dr. Chapman's practical guidance empowers readers to break free from the chains of emotional turmoil and experience true freedom. Highly recommended!"

Matt Rocco, CEO of Etech Global Services

"Dr. Chapman has an incredible talent of teaching us how to use our faith and effective treatment skills in tandem to address our emotions. This text outlines the skills we are meant to have from a biblical perspective while simultaneously providing concrete skills rooted in cognitive behavioral therapy. The clear biblical and therapeutic guidance is easy to follow, and the practice questions and prompts following each section allow you to see how to put your new knowledge into practice! I highly recommend this book for all believers who are hoping to gain clear skills to manage emotions."

Elizabeth McIngvale, licensed clinical social worker and director of the OCD Institute of Texas

"I am nearer to God and more at home in myself after reading *Mastering Our Emotions*. This book is a tool, companion, and guide. Personally, I've struggled to accept my emotions and my tendency to be emotional. Kevin Chapman's writing helped me to move past acceptance of my emotional self into understanding of and love for my emotions. Reading this book will help any person respond to their emotions with confidence. Engaging in the exercises in this book will help any person leverage emotions toward a deeper intimacy with our Intelligent Designer."

Darrell E. Hall, author of *Speaking Across Generations* and pastor of The Way Community Church in Conyers, Georgia

DR. KEVIN CHAPMAN

MASTERING
OUR
EMOTIONS

😆 😄 😲 😠

BIBLICAL PRINCIPLES
FOR EMOTIONAL HEALTH

ívp

An imprint of InterVarsity Press
Downers Grove, Illinois

InterVarsity Press
P.O. Box 1400 | Downers Grove, IL 60515-1426
ivpress.com | email@ivpress.com

InterVarsity Press® is the publishing division of InterVarsity Christian Fellowship/USA®. For more information, visit intervarsity.org.

All Scripture quotations, unless otherwise indicated, are taken from The New King James Version®. Copyright © 1982 by Thomas Nelson, Inc. Used by permission. All rights reserved.

While any stories in this book are true, some names and identifying information may have been changed to protect the privacy of individuals.

The publisher cannot verify the accuracy or functionality of website URLs used in this book beyond the date of publication.

Cover design: David Fassett
Interior design: Daniel van Loon
Images: iStock / Getty Images Plus: ©akinbostanci, ©Barmaleeva

ISBN 978-1-5140-1057-0 (print) | ISBN 978-1-5140-1058-7 (digital)

Printed in the United States of America ♾

Library of Congress Cataloging-in-Publication Data
Names: Chapman, Kevin (Psychologist), author.
Title: Mastering our emotions : biblical principles for emotional health /
   Dr. Kevin Chapman.
Description: Downers Grove, IL : IVP, [2024] | Includes bibliographical
   references.
Identifiers: LCCN 2024028298 (print) | LCCN 2024028299 (ebook) | ISBN
   9781514010570 (print) | ISBN 9781514010587 (digital)
Subjects: LCSH: Emotions–Religious aspects–Christianity. |
   Emotions–Biblical teaching. | BISAC: RELIGION / Christian Living /
   Personal Growth | SELF-HELP / Emotions
Classification: LCC BS680.E4 C43 2024 (print) | LCC BS680.E4 (ebook) |
   DDC 248.401/9–dc23/eng/20240708
LC record available at https://lccn.loc.gov/2024028298
LC ebook record available at https://lccn.loc.gov/2024028299

31   30   29   28   27   26 | 12   11   10   9   8   7   6   5   4   3

TO THE READER

God has designed us to experience emotions, as Jesus experienced the same emotions. However, as born-again believers, we are not designed to be dominated by emotions. We are designed to regulate emotions and respond to any circumstance in an adaptive fashion that we "may prove what *is* that good and acceptable and perfect will of God" in all situations (Romans 12:2).

CONTENTS

INTRODUCTION

Now may the God of peace Himself sanctify you completely;
and may your whole spirit, soul, and body be preserved
blameless at the coming of our Lord Jesus Christ.

1 THESSALONIANS 5:23

D o you ever struggle with being anxious when the Bible tells us not to be anxious? Do you struggle with managing your thoughts when the Bible tells us to take our thoughts captive? Do you struggle with public speaking or interacting with others when the Bible tells us that "the fear of man brings a snare" (Proverbs 29:25)? Do you struggle with air travel, crowds, or other situations involving feeling trapped when the Bible tells us that God has not given us a spirit of fear? Do you struggle with chronic worry about a number of events or activities in your daily life when the Bible tells us not to worry about any of these situations? As believers, many of us have likely experienced a significant discrepancy between who the Bible says we are in Jesus and who we believe we are due to our emotional experiences.

First Thessalonians 5:23 makes it clear that we are a three-part being: spirt, soul, and body. God has designed every human on earth with these three parts, with our spirit being the component of our identity that relates to God since God is spirit (John 4:24). Moreover, our soul contains the mental and emotional facets of our identities and is essential in directing our attention to the Word of God. It is here, in the soul, where people struggle with their relationship with God and their relationships with those around them, often due to difficulties with managing emotions. Though the Word of God tells us that we "may prove what *is* that good and acceptable and perfect will of God" through renewing our minds (Romans 12:2), I find that the large majority of people who I see clinically or personally in church, who profess to be believers, struggle with the practical application of doing so.

This manual represents a merger of two schools of thought that have historically been viewed as diametrically opposed to one another: the Word of God (the Bible) and the science of psychology, specifically cognitive-behavioral therapy (CBT) and affective neuroscience. Interestingly, through my exploration as a Christian and a clinical psychologist, I have learned that these two schools of thought reflect similar principles that share more commonalities than disparities. As such, the Lord has placed an unwavering desire within me to assist fellow Christians in understanding the following: the role and function of emotions, the mysteries of the soul, and God's divine purpose as it pertains to managing emotions so that we may be effective in witnessing to others while prospering as our souls prosper (3 John 1:2). I have found that the emotional regulation skills and the kingdom principles in this guide will allow you to reprogram your experiences with emotions and fulfill the destiny that God has called you to.

Central to this manual is understanding the role of a certain part of temperament known as *neuroticism*, which can be understood as experiencing negative emotions frequently and intensely. It is important to note that this temperament label is simply to help you understand the concept of negative emotions (rather than to diagnose a problem). Temperament is not black and white;

we all vary to some degree in different facets of temperament. For example, I am mostly extroverted when around groups of people, but I appear introverted when working out at a gym. Just like extroversion refers to a tendency to experience positive emotions and to be interpersonally warm and social, individuals high in neuroticism have a tendency toward experiencing negative emotions and view negative emotions as dangerous.

As I'll explore further in this manual, I believe a tendency toward negative emotionality is one of the emotional consequences of the fall, and this is why many believers continue to struggle with negative emotions. The events in the Garden of Eden explain much of the difficulty we have experienced in our souls and bodies. In addition to Adam's and Eve's eyes being opened to evil in the world during the fall, the door for a predisposition to high neuroticism, or the tendency to experience negative emotions while perceiving the world as threatening and being unable to cope with it, was also opened.

In the physical realm, people who struggle with negative emotions continue to do so for two interrelated reasons: (1) They have negative views of emotions, such as viewing negative emotions as dangerous and believing that one must get rid of them. This leads to (2) avoidant behaviors that are aimed at eliminating the negative emotions. These behaviors may provide temporary relief from the negative emotions; however, they eventually backfire and lead to a continuation of negative and often intense emotions.

Though there are a number of natural consequences that have occurred as the result of the fall, this book is most concerned with what we consider to be the *emotional* consequence—the tendency to experience high levels of neuroticism or chronic distress in the soul. The process of intense negative emotions becomes a vicious cycle of attempting to push emotions away, which in turn leads to a continuation of the emotions, creating what we call *soul distress*. Soul distress represents emotional

A MODEL OF EMOTIONAL DISTRESS FOR CHRISTIANS

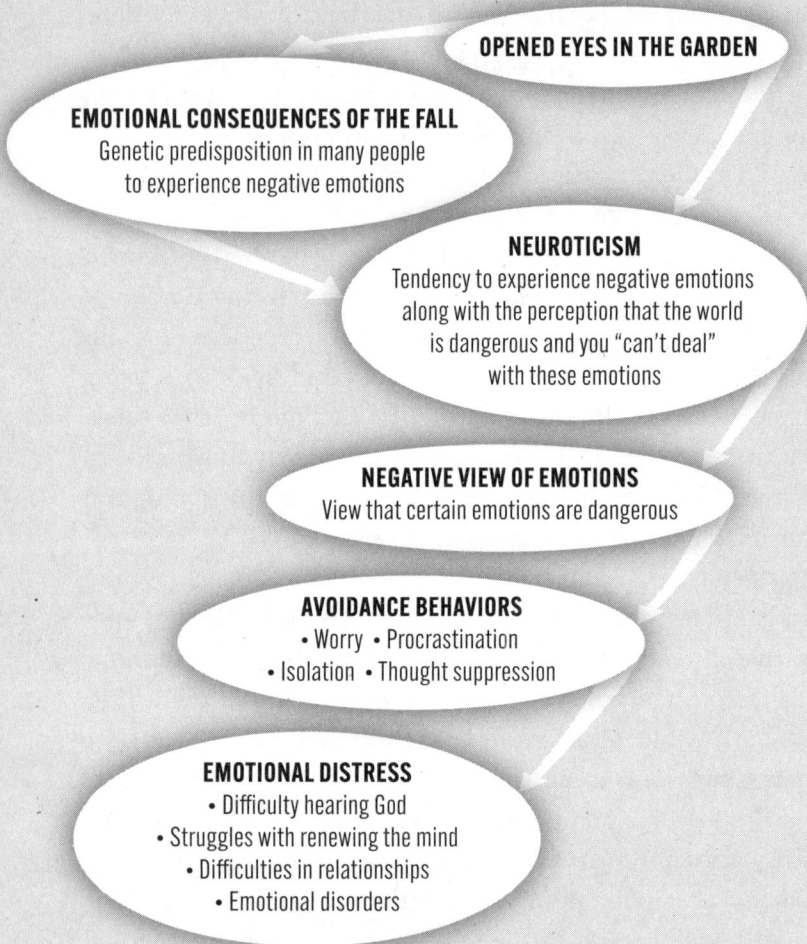

OPENED EYES IN THE GARDEN

EMOTIONAL CONSEQUENCES OF THE FALL
Genetic predisposition in many people
to experience negative emotions

NEUROTICISM
Tendency to experience negative emotions
along with the perception that the world
is dangerous and you "can't deal"
with these emotions

NEGATIVE VIEW OF EMOTIONS
View that certain emotions are dangerous

AVOIDANCE BEHAVIORS
• Worry • Procrastination
• Isolation • Thought suppression

EMOTIONAL DISTRESS
• Difficulty hearing God
• Struggles with renewing the mind
• Difficulties in relationships
• Emotional disorders

difficulties in our lives, including struggles within our relationships. These struggles range from minor problems in our relationship with God and our relationships with others on one end
of the spectrum, to diagnosable emotional disorders on the other
end. In regard to our relationship with God, it makes sense why

many believers struggle in this area, because the soul is the part of our makeup where we actively shift our attention to God or the world. When soul distress hinders us from putting our attention on God, it often leads us to perceive our relationship with God as weak, and emotional victory in the Christian life as impossible.

The skills within this manual are divided into seven key principles that are explained throughout each chapter. These "being skills" need to be practiced regularly in addition to renewing your mind with the accompanying Scriptures throughout these chapters. These seven "being skills" are as follows:

1. Being an Emotional Master
2. Being Present
3. Being Renewed
4. Being Adaptive
5. Being Physical
6. Being Brave
7. Being Consistent

HOW TO USE THIS MANUAL

This manual has been written for flexible application to both individuals and groups. It is highly recommended that you read each chapter on your own and apply the content within each chapter on a weekly basis. The skills within this manual are designed to initially increase your awareness of emotions so that you can then apply these skills to day-to-day situations. I have found in my experience that you will receive the most benefit from this manual if you read each chapter and focus on it for one week at a time, prior to moving on to the next section. This manual is designed so that you can carefully read each chapter, meditate on the Scriptures contained throughout, objectively record your answers to the reflection questions, and apply the "being skills" to your life.

WHO IS THIS MANUAL DESIGNED FOR?

If you are a pastor, small group leader, Bible study leader, or any other group facilitator within your areas of spiritual influence, this manual can be applied in a similar fashion with the added advantage of group accountability. If utilized in a group setting, I recommend you begin each week by reviewing homework from the previous week, which will facilitate group discussion. The reflection questions and exercises throughout each chapter can also be used as prompts for group discussion. Additionally, if you are using this manual in a group setting, I suggest you help each other confront uncomfortable situations and practice the "being skills."

If you practice these skills on a regular basis, you will learn to master your emotions, improve your relationships with others, and most importantly, enhance your relationship with God. Welcome to *Mastering Our Emotions*!

If you are using *Mastering Our Emotions* in a group or ministry setting, scan this QR code to download a PDF featuring larger, printable versions of some of the worksheets in this book.

1

IN THE BEGINNING

In the beginning God created the heavens and the earth.

GENESIS 1:1

M any believers are familiar with this first verse of the Bible and the story of creation. However, in Genesis 3 something else was "created" that was not part of God's original plan, nor did he create it. It is one of the many results from the fall, and it forms the basis for this book to managing emotions as a believer.

In Genesis 3 we see the heading for the chapter, titled "The Temptation and Fall of Man." Again, many believers are familiar with the story of Adam and Eve, the role of the serpent, and the bites that are taken of the fruit from the tree of the knowledge of good and evil. Rarely, however, do we think about the *emotional consequences* that occurred because of this act of disobedience by Adam and Eve. This one act set the course for millions of people to struggle with managing the emotions that God originally designed for our benefit. I've personally encountered thousands of people, including many believers, who struggle with managing anxiety, anger, sadness, fear, shame, and disgust, and who have become comfortable with being uncomfortable. I have studied the family transmission of anxiety as a clinical psychologist. I have treated thousands of individuals with anxiety disorders (phobias, chronic worry, social anxiety disorder, panic disorder, and agoraphobia), depression, obsessive-compulsive disorder, posttraumatic stress disorder, suicidal ideation, and countless other mental health conditions. I have witnessed people use emotional avoidance in its many forms as a coping mechanism in vain attempts to manage negative emotions. I have seen countless individuals quote 2 Timothy 1:7, "For God has not given us a spirit of fear, but of power and of love and of a sound mind," as well as Philippians 4:6, "Be anxious for nothing," yet still be dominated by emotional experiences despite what they know to be true from God's Word. I have observed numerous believers declare that God has delivered us from the power of darkness and that we are strengthened with all might, as noted in Colossians 1:9-14, yet still struggle with negative emotionality. In short, the most knowledgeable believers are often still dominated by their souls (i.e., emotional experiences) due to a lack of practical understanding of what occurred during the temptation and fall of humans.

THE TEMPTATION AND FALL

Our journey begins in Genesis 3:6-10:

> So when the woman saw that the tree *was* good for food, that it *was* pleasant to the eyes, and a tree desirable to make *one* wise, she took of its fruit and ate. She also gave to her husband with her, and he ate. Then the eyes of both of them were opened, and they knew that they *were* naked; and they sewed fig leaves together and made themselves coverings.
>
> And they heard the sound of the LORD God walking in the garden in the cool of the day, and Adam and his wife hid themselves from the presence of the LORD God among the trees of the garden.

Then the LORD God called to Adam and said to him, "Where *are* you?"

So he said, "I heard Your voice in the garden, and I was afraid because I was naked; and I hid myself."

Though we understand the temptation and fall of humans as a significant event that would change the history of humankind, we often miss a very important aspect of what occurred from an emotional standpoint: the fall gave rise to the temperament trait known as *neuroticism*. As noted in the introduction, individuals who are high in this trait tend to experience intense, negative emotions. Just like many of us are high in extraversion, which refers to a tendency to experience positive emotions and to be warm toward others, those of us who are high in neuroticism tend to view negative emotions as dangerous and intolerable. In essence, high neuroticism is linked to emotional disorder diagnoses such as panic disorder, major depressive disorder, and social anxiety disorder.[1]

In Genesis, we can observe three traits of neuroticism. First, the revelation of nakedness causes shame and embarrassment. This was never intended by God. Although this manual will primarily address negative emotionality due to its impact on our functioning as believers, the fall also negatively contributed to our low expression of positive emotion, which has also created negative consequences. Low expression of positive mood as a result of the fall may affect our expression of the fruit of the Spirit, how we express hopefulness (in contrast to hopelessness), as well as our enjoyment of activities and relationships. God did not intend for us to believe that we must hide. Adam and Eve "knew that they *were* naked," and experienced shame and embarrassment because of this new knowledge, and therefore, "sewed fig leaves together and made themselves coverings" (Genesis 3:7).

Second, we see the first experience of *anxiety* in the Bible. Adam and Eve hid themselves from the presence of God when "they heard the sound of the LORD God walking in the garden in the cool of the day" (Genesis 3:8). Notice it says that they "*heard* the sound of the Lord God walking" as opposed to "they *saw* the Lord God walking." This implies that they experienced distress in anticipation of seeing God in the (near) future because they believed their encounter with him would result in a negative outcome, which is the essence of the emotion of anxiety.

Third, we see the first experience of the emotion known as *fear* in the Bible. When God was speaking directly to Adam and Eve, they experienced distress in response to what they viewed as present danger, which is the essence of fear. Ironically, we were never intended to experience these negative emotions in the presence of our Creator, yet Adam and Eve's emotional responses to God revealed the magnitude of an extremely negative consequence from the temptation and fall of man: the birth of high levels of neuroticism. Though research on emotional disorders indicates that heightened levels of neuroticism is a primary risk factor for developing an emotional disorder, it is also something that can be changed through the application of kingdom principles and the science of psychology.

THE BIRTH OF EMOTIONAL DISTRESS

The emotional effects of the fall have had a persisting impact on all of humankind. Despite whether you personally struggle with negative emotionality, the consequences of Adam and Eve partaking of the fruit from the tree of the knowledge of good and evil are easily observable: wars, rumors of wars, difficulties within parent-child relationships, and the staggering statistics on emotional disorders. The shame, fear, and anxiety that were initially manifested in the Garden of Eden are among the primary negative emotional experiences that so many believers struggle with today.

Along these lines, consider for a moment the following questions: Do you struggle with worry about minor matters or perhaps worry about things that might happen in the future?

Have you ever experienced a panic attack? Do you "clam up" when you are in social situations and become extremely uncomfortable when you must be in front of others? Do you dislike tight spaces? Do you often worry about your health and become uncomfortable when you experience unknown bodily sensations? Do you check Google when you feel a "twinge" in your body, hoping to find answers? Maybe you feel down and depressed while finding it difficult to enjoy activities that you used to enjoy. Do you experience "scary" thoughts that come into your mind, that then lead you to seek reassurance from others or attempt to block thoughts that may seem contrary to the Word of God? Do you "fly off the handle" over what other people would consider small things? Do you have a difficult time tolerating the unknown? Or maybe you avoid situations because they seem to trigger uncomfortable feelings in your body. Do you lie awake at night because of your thoughts? Do you have a difficult time praying or hearing from God due to your mind wandering to either the future or the past?

If you answered yes to any of these questions, do these symptoms cause you personal distress or impairment in everyday functioning (e.g., work, school, relationships, church, or social activities)? Some examples of distress and impairment in functioning include not being able to speak up in group settings out of fear of negative evaluation, not being assertive, missing out on leisure activities due to anxiety or depression, frequent panic attacks, your sleep being disrupted on a regular basis due to not being able to turn off your thoughts, or avoiding places and situations altogether due to feeling uncomfortable.

If you struggle in any capacity with what I just mentioned, then perhaps the tendency toward negative emotionality that initially occurred in the Garden of Eden is the culprit. Even if you are not high in this tendency to experience "big feelings" but some of these situations are difficult to manage, then you will benefit from this manual.

UNDERSTANDING EMOTIONAL DISTRESS

As we noted earlier in this chapter, some individuals struggle with the tendency to experience negative emotions coupled with the perception that the world around them is dangerous and that they are ill-equipped to deal with it. This tendency toward experiencing intense emotions was first evidenced in the Garden of Eden and explains why many of us struggle with the questions mentioned earlier. There is an abundance of research literature that suggests that neuroticism emotionality is among one of the most important risk factors for developing an emotional disorder, particularly for anxiety disorders and depression. Most importantly, this tendency can be reprogrammed. To understand how to reprogram symptoms of emotional distress that are both created and maintained by high levels of neuroticism, we must first understand the role that emotions play in our lives and what they are made of. Doing so will allow us to practice the skills taught in later chapters that have proven to change lives.

REFLECTION: IN THE BEGINNING

Read Genesis 3:1-21.

1. In verse 7 of Genesis 3, what happened emotionally when Adam and Eve "knew that they were naked"? Describe it in your own words.

2. How did Adam and Eve's perception of God change in Genesis 3:8 when "they heard the sound of the LORD God walking in the garden in the cool of the day"?

3. Has the fall and the resulting sin that entered the world impacted your experience with emotions? What are some specific examples in your life?

HOMEWORK

1. *Read* Colossians 1:9-14 and pray the prayer found in that passage once per day for the next week during your time with the Lord. Make note of anything that stands out to you or that God reveals to you during your prayer time.

2. *Pray:* Ask the Holy Spirit to give you wisdom and revelation about how the fall has affected how you've experienced emotions over time. Ask him during your prayer time to reveal to you how to pray for your family if they have struggled with mastering emotions.

3. *Read* Genesis 3 and ask God to reveal to you the areas of your life where negative emotions have been viewed as dangerous. Record those areas below.

2

BEING AN EMOTIONAL MASTER

THE PURPOSE OF YOUR EMOTIONS

A fool vents all his feelings,
But a wise man holds them back.

PROVERBS 29:11

As we discussed in chapter one, intense emotionality began in the Garden of Eden. You will soon learn throughout this manual that our emotions are important and help us make sense of the world around us. Further, we see several biblical examples of emotions being a part of the regular experiences of God's people, both negative and positive, as well as instructions on how to respond to many of these emotions.

Despite the Word of God providing both reference to and instructions on the importance of matters of the soul, we often struggle to relate these biblical experiences of negative emotions to negative emotions of our own. In doing so, we sometimes create and apply religious terms to emotions that we deem as destructive or damaging because we don't understand the nature and function of the emotions. The best example is found in John 2:13-17 when Jesus made a whip of cords and drove out the money changers. Most believers would agree that Jesus experienced anger in this instance. However, because we are taught that anger is negative and destructive, we have a difficult time reconciling how Jesus, who was without sin, could be angry. In an attempt to explain Jesus' anger, some label his anger as "righteous anger." As noted in Ephesians 4:26 and Psalm 4:4, "Be angry, and do not sin" clarifies that anger is necessary at times and should be navigated without sinful actions. However, as it relates to Jesus in the temple, was the anger itself actually righteous, and did Jesus righteously and adaptively respond to his emotion of anger, which was based on the context?

In other words, there are moral reasons as Christians that we *should* experience anger, as in the case of Jesus in the temple and when our Christian beliefs are violated, but there are also other valid reasons to experience anger such as when you or a loved one have been intentionally harmed by someone, regardless of morality. This distinction becomes extremely important if you have learned to only view anger as valid if it is righteous, since other events will trigger anger and require an equally important response. In sum, anger is not the problem, but rather, the response to anger can be.

Many of us also experience intense emotions of sadness and anxiety. In Mark 14:32-36, when Jesus prayed in the garden of Gethsemane shortly before he was betrayed, he was "troubled and deeply distressed," his soul was "exceedingly sorrowful," and he initially asked the Father to take the cup from him. It is clear that Jesus was both sad and anxious. He felt the same emotions we do, which are normal parts of our experiences as believers. Many of us, however, frequently struggle with experiencing negative emotions that result in behaviors we often regret due to our difficulty with responding "righteously" to the emotions. In other words, experiencing emotions is a normal part of our existence, but we are not to be dominated by our emotions. For us to reprogram our tendency to experience negative emotions frequently and uncomfortably, and to respond to them in adaptive and righteous ways, we must understand the purpose (or function) of emotions and their three components.

THE PURPOSE OF EMOTIONS

The purpose of an emotion is to prompt us to respond to both internal events (thoughts or physical sensations) and external situations. Emotions trigger us to pay attention to things going on inside of us, as well as around us, so we can respond to the world successfully. Furthermore, although many people are uncomfortable with experiencing negative emotions, both positive and negative emotions are equally important to pay attention to.

If someone were to say, "You are so emotional," you could respond by saying, "You are too." Everyone is emotional, yet many people who experience negative emotions more frequently (i.e., high trait neuroticism) tend to be described as "so emotional" or "too emotional." Consider for a moment if we didn't have emotions. How would you experience the joy of the Lord during praise and worship? How would you be assertive and stand up for yourself? How would you deal with the loss of a loved one, a pet, or something important to you? How would you survive in a fire? How would you know if you ate food that was contaminated? If you failed to keep your word to a friend, how would you know? Let's explore emotions and why they are necessary for our survival.

FEAR

The Word tells us in Joshua 1:9 and Deuteronomy 31:6 that we are to "be strong and of good courage," not fear, and that the Lord is with us. What is the difference between having a spirit of fear and experiencing natural physical symptoms of fear that science can help us understand? Let's explore these concepts.

One of the most misunderstood emotions in Christians is the emotion known as fear. The Greek word for "fear" is *phobos* (where we get the word *phobia*) and refers to that which causes flight, terror, or dread. Fear is what is known as "fight, flight, or freeze" and is your body's response to situations that pose a real present danger or threat. We often react to situations with the fear response without even thinking. The fear response includes increased heart rate, dilated pupils, and increased blood flow to your core so that you may take effective action to fight danger, flee a dangerous situation, or freeze if movement would possibly lead to death (e.g., facing a vicious animal or having to be still during a hostage situation).[1] Though uncomfortable, you can see why fear is important for navigating danger.

Based on the body's natural alarm reaction to real danger, the research literature refers to panic attacks as the clinical manifestation of fear, also known as a "false alarm." The reason a panic attack is considered a false alarm is because there is no actual danger in the situation but the person having the attack experiences the fight, flight, or freeze response because they interpret the situation as dangerous. One example is feeling trapped (interpreting the situation as inescapable and dangerous) in a crowded place and therefore having a panic attack. Though one could construe many intense negative emotions that occur in the context of perceived danger, such as anger or shame, science confirms that panic attacks represent the epitome of a "false alarm" due to perceived mortal danger.[2]

Though the Bible often uses the terms *fear* and *anxiety* interchangeably, it is helpful to distinguish between these two emotional experiences for several reasons. God's Word tells us to "fear not." One interpretation of "fear not" is to work toward not responding to situations by having a panic attack when the situations are not in fact dangerous, but rather to trust that the Lord is with us in these situations. On the other hand, when experiencing real danger, we can remember both that the Lord remains with us and that our emotional response of fear is appropriate for escape or facing the danger. (For more discussion of fear in Scripture, see Deuteronomy 3:22; 31:6; Joshua 1:9; Judges 6:23; 2 Kings 6:16; Isaiah 41:10; 41:13; Joel 2:21; Matthew 10:31; John 12:15; 2 Timothy 1:7; and 1 John 4:18.)

ANXIETY

Anxiety in the heart of man causes depression, but a good word makes it glad.

Proverbs 12:25

Be anxious for nothing, but in everything by prayer and supplication, with thanksgiving, let your requests be made known to God; and the peace of God, which surpasses all understanding, will guard your hearts and minds through Christ Jesus.

Philippians 4:6-7

There are two important takeaways from Proverbs 12:25 and Philippians 4:6-7 worth noting. First, anxiety and depression occur together at such high rates that many of the symptoms of both look the same. Second, the treatment for both requires changing thinking patterns to reflect truth ("a good word") and shifting attention to positive cues. We will talk more about these concepts later.

The word *anxiety* comes from the Greek word *merimna*, which means "that which causes distracting care." Anxiety is an emotion that helps us prepare for future events such as an upcoming meeting, a presentation, or a test. Anxiety equips us to shift our attention away from what is happening in the present moment so that we may engage in behaviors that will help us avoid negative outcomes in the future. Examples include studying to prevent failing a test, rehearsing lines to present the right content, and practicing to ensure that we perform well. Imagine if you did not study for an upcoming test or prepare for a job interview. Again, anxiety is useful when we respond to it adaptively.

Just like fear, however, when anxiety occurs too frequently, is out of proportion to the actual threat, is difficult to manage in the situation, lasts longer than the situation calls for, causes us to lose sight of its intended purpose, or prevents us from experiencing the peace of God, it typically leads to avoidance strategies that serve as futile attempts to manage it. Chronic anxiety has a number of manifestations in our thoughts, physical sensations, and behaviors. Examples include frequent panic attacks that are driven by thoughts of danger; headaches, muscle tension, and sleep disruption as a result of chronic worry; and avoidance behaviors due to unrealistic thoughts that situations are dangerous, as well as being overly protective toward our children. It should be noted that chronic anxiety can be transmitted from parent to children through modeling behaviors and communicating to children that situations are dangerous. The Word of God has much to say about the emotional experience of anxiety. (For more discussion of anxiety in Scripture, see Psalm 94:19; Proverbs 12:25; and Philippians 4:6-7.)

IS A "SPIRIT OF FEAR" DESCRIBING ANXIETY OR FEAR?

Since fear is in response to present danger, and anxiety is in response to future danger, the million-dollar question for many believers is, What does it mean to have a "spirit of fear"? Though the concept of a spirit of fear is subject to many different interpretations, based on my study of the Bible and my experience with clients, a spirit of fear can be defined as any emotional pattern of chronic fearfulness that creates emotional distress, negative interpretations of emotions and the situations that surround these emotions, and emotional responses that are not helpful for the situation. In other words, many of the chronic manifestations of the emotional patterns described throughout this manual can be interpreted as a spirit of fear.

ANGER

> When He had made a whip of cords, He drove them all out of the temple, with the sheep and the oxen, and poured out the changers' money and overturned the tables.
>
> John 2:15

> "Be angry, and do not sin": do not let the sun go down on your wrath.
>
> Ephesians 4:26

There is much that we can learn from Jesus' experience with anger and Paul's description of it. In fact, God gave us the emotion of anger for our benefit: both David (Psalm 4:4) and Paul (Ephesians 4:26) tell us to be angry but not to sin in the process of being angry. You would be hard-pressed to argue against the notion that Jesus' anger was appropriate, considering what was happening in the temple. Along these lines, anger is a natural response when we or a loved one has been wronged or slighted in some way (e.g., Jesus in the temple), or when a goal-directed behavior has been blocked by someone. Anger, however, is not always in response to someone else's actions; it can also be triggered by the perception that one's concept of fairness has been violated, and the anger may not be directed toward a person but to a source. For example, we may become angry at an organization because we have had negative experiences in the past with individuals within the organization. We can also think of anger as an adaptive response when a person knowingly and intentionally acts in a hurtful way toward us or someone we care about.

Anger prompts us to defend ourselves and protect our loved ones. Anger itself is frequently stereotyped as a destructive emotion, when people's response to anger is often what is actually destructive. Chronic expressions of anger such as swearing, yelling at another driver on the road, screaming at your children, giving your spouse the silent treatment, and physical aggression toward objects or people are common examples of destructive responses to anger. Spiritually, we usually think of the destructive response to anger as wrath (Proverbs 15:1; Ephesians 4:31), and the adaptive response to anger as righteous. An adaptive response refers to a response that allows you to pay attention to what the emotion is trying to indicate and results in taking effective action in a given situation. As we noted earlier with Jesus in the temple, he responded to the money changers' behaviors in God's house (mistreatment of the temple) in an adaptive fashion; not only did he assert his authority in the temple, but he also established through his actions an explicit code of conduct for anyone who would ever interface with the house of God. In other words, Jesus' response to anger was both *righteous* and *adaptive*.

In modern-day society, how would you respond if your cable company failed to tell you about hidden fees? What if a teacher shamed your daughter in front of the entire class, prompting her to cry as soon as she got in the car? Anger prompts you to take effective action by being assertive, which is what Jesus did in the temple. The Word of God has much to say about the emotional experience of anger. (For more discussion of anger in Scripture, see Psalm 4:4; 37:8; Proverbs 15:1; 16:32; 19:11; Matthew 5:22; John 2:15; and Ephesians 4:26.)

SADNESS

Better to go to the house of mourning
Than to go to the house of feasting,
For that is the end of all men;
And the living will take it to heart.
Sorrow is better than laughter,
For by a sad countenance the heart is made better.

Ecclesiastes 7:2-3

Contrary to what many people learn to believe, God gave us the emotion of sadness for our benefit. Specifically, sadness is a natural emotional response to loss or to a setback in our lives that is important to us, such as losing a job, the ending of a season in our lives, or the death of a loved one. Unlike the other emotions that we have discussed, sadness creates a sense of heaviness and lack of energy to prompt us to take a step back or withdraw so we may reflect on the loss, gather our resources, and move forward with our lives following the loss or setback. For example, if someone becomes sad after a divorce, that sadness is designed to help them take a step back, reflect on the relationship, and process what went wrong. If that individual were to jump into another marriage without reflecting on the previous one, they would be avoiding the emotion of sadness, which could cause them to repeat the same mistakes in the new relationship and spiral into more sadness.

The emotional disorder that serves as chronic sadness is known as *depression*. Depression is the chronic experience of sadness that creates significant distress and impairment in functioning as a result of a number of other symptoms that accompany sadness, including anhedonia (lack of interest in pleasurable activities), fatigue, feelings of worthlessness, excessive and inappropriate guilt, sleep disturbance, difficulty concentrating, and suicidal ideation. (Always seek the guidance of a mental health professional if experiencing suicidal ideation.) As noted earlier in the manual, the skills that follow are designed not only to reduce the symptoms of emotional disorders but also to reprogram your tendency to respond to emotions in a negative fashion (i.e., reprogramming neuroticism). The Word of God has much to say about the emotional experience of sadness. (For more discussion of sadness in Scripture, see Ecclesiastes 1:18; 7:2-3; Psalm 34:18; 42:6; Proverbs 12:25; Isaiah 53:4; Mark 10:22; 14:33-35; Romans 9:2; and 2 Corinthians 7:10.)

GUILT AND SHAME

Guilt and shame are emotional responses to falling short of a personally significant standard. *Guilt* often results from falling short of moral or societal standards in our behavior. For example, if you promised a loved one that you would visit them in the hospital when they became ill but failed to do so, guilt would prompt you to apologize and make it up to the person upon discharge. *Shame* occurs when we fail to meet a personal standard and feel "less than others" as a result. Shame usually reflects a deeper, negative perception of ourselves in relation to others. For example, if I broke a team rule and it resulted in my entire team getting in trouble, shame could be the emotional response. Like sadness, shame prompts us to withdraw from others to process what occurred and make amends. It is important to note that both guilt and shame serve a God-given purpose. When responded to correctly, guilt and shame can help us improve our relationships and work harder in areas of our lives.

However, chronic guilt and shame, which often have multiple causes, can have devastating consequences. Spiritually, we must be careful with the emotions of guilt and shame. Chronic guilt can be similar to condemnation, which Romans 8:1 speaks against for the believer. Being "contrite" (i.e., convicted by the Holy Spirit) on the other hand, would be the godly/adaptive response to an emotion such as guilt. The Word of God has much to say about the emotions of guilt and shame, particularly the godly responses toward guilt and shame. (For more discussion of guilt and shame in Scripture, see Psalm 34:18; 40:15; 51:17; 69:19; 71:1; 89:45; Proverbs 12:16; 13:5; Jeremiah 13:26; Habakkuk 2:16; and Romans 10:11.)

DISGUST

But that we write to them to abstain from things polluted by idols, from sexual immorality, from things strangled, and from blood.

Acts 15:20

Disgust is a natural emotional response to contamination. Contamination can include both physical (e.g., a stomach bug) and
moral (e.g., things in the world that are morally repulsive) types.
It is easy for us to understand the important response of vomiting
when we have a stomach bug so that we can eliminate a foreign
substance from our bodies. I see many clients who have what is
known as emetophobia, or the fear of vomiting, and other clients
who struggle with unrealistic fears of both moral and physical
contamination as in the case of OCD, which has an anxiety component. We often fail to realize, however, that God designed us
to experience disgust in response to moral contamination. For
example, my wife has a strong physical reaction in response to TV
ads that violate our moral beliefs. Ironically, like the other emotions we've discussed, God designed us to be aware of the spiritual danger of contamination just like he designed us to navigate
physical contamination. The Word of God has much to say about
the emotion of disgust. (For more discussion of contamination
in Scripture, see Numbers 35:33; Psalm 106:38; Ecclesiastes 10:1;
Isaiah 19:6; Jeremiah 2:23; Ezekiel 34:19; Zephaniah 3:1; 2 Peter
2:20; and Revelation 16:2.)

REFLECTION: UNDERSTANDING THE PURPOSE OF EMOTIONS

1. How has your understanding of fear versus anxiety changed
after reading this chapter?

2. In your own words, describe the difference between fear and
anxiety. Write one example of when you experienced fear and
one example of when you experienced anxiety below.

Fear:

Anxiety:

3. Give an example of when you experienced anger and responded to it appropriately.

4. Have you ever experienced moral disgust? Give an example.

5. *Read* Ecclesiastes 7:2-3. What does this suggest about the emotion of sadness?

6. Describe a time when you experienced guilt and a time when you experienced shame. What did you learn?

1. **Read** some of the Scriptures listed with each emotion in this chapter. Write down any revelations you receive about specific emotions that apply to you and your experiences with these emotions.

2. **Pray:** Ask the Holy Spirit to give you wisdom and revelation about emotions that you have viewed as threatening, have tried to push away, or did not understand.

3

BEING AN EMOTIONAL MASTER

THE PARTS OF YOUR EMOTIONS

Then He spoke a parable to them, saying: "The ground of a certain
rich man yielded plentifully. And he thought within himself, saying,
'What shall I do, since I have no room to store my crops?' So he said,
'I will do this: I will pull down my barns and build greater, and there
I will store all my crops and my goods. And I will say to my soul,
"Soul, you have many goods laid up for many years; take your ease;
eat, drink, and be merry."'"

LUKE 12:16-19

L uke 12:16-19 is from Jesus' parable of the rich fool—in Jesus'
depiction of the process by which the foolish rich man decided he would lay up treasures for himself, we see an accurate description of the way many of us make many decisions on
a regular basis. The process by which the rich man decided to lay
up treasures began with an initial *thought*. The passage goes on
to indicate that the rich man spoke to his soul, meaning he was
having an internal dialogue with himself. Though this Scripture
does not imply that the rich man pulled down his barns and built
greater ones, it does indicate that his thoughts were intended to

lead to the *behaviors* of doing so. Additionally, having thoughts of any kind is accompanied by physical sensations that prepare our bodies to engage in a behavior that is consistent with the initial thought. Understanding this emotional process is central to becoming an emotional master as a believer since it is impossible to apply skills to manage emotions more effectively if we are unaware of the parts of our emotional experiences.

THE THREE PARTS OF EMOTIONS: THE EMOTIONAL TRIAD

Think of your emotions as a triad: all emotions, both positive and negative, have three parts. Historically, most people have described emotions as feelings, but feelings are only one of the three parts of emotions. When we describe emotions as feelings (e.g., "I feel like you shouldn't have said that to me!"), we are often unable to articulate the actual emotion associated with the event. By understanding that all emotions have three parts, you will create the necessary foundation that will allow you to effectively manage your emotions in any situation while enhancing your relationships with God and those around you.

THE THREE PARTS OF AN EMOTION

THOUGHTS
What am I thinking?

PHYSICAL SENSATIONS
What am I feeling in my body?

BEHAVIORS
What am I doing / what do I feel like doing?

PART ONE: THOUGHTS—WHAT YOU SAY TO YOURSELF
OR WHAT YOU THINK ABOUT A SITUATION

How you feel about a situation is directly influenced by what you say to yourself / what you think about the situation. Unfortunately, most people are unaware of their thoughts and instead focus on the feelings in their bodies. For example, one Sunday morning you walk into a new church and see that the praise and worship has already started. The nice greeter at the door escorts you and your family to a section of the church that requires you to enter a row full of people. You might imagine that this is an anxiety-provoking situation for most people, but your thoughts (such as *This is so awkward*, or *I don't know anyone*), not the situation itself, are what create the emotion known as anxiety. On the other hand, you may enter the same situation and say to yourself, *The joy of the Lord is in this place!* In this case you will probably feel invigorated and excited because of what you said to yourself. Notice in both of these situations you are arriving after praise and worship has started and being escorted to a row full of people. The situation did not change, and the arousal or physical sensations in your body did not change; however, how you interpreted the physical sensations in your body / what you were thinking did change. That interpretation of the physical sensations in your body further influences and intensifies the emotional experience. That is why our interpretation/thoughts are so important.

REFLECTION: UNDERSTANDING THE PARTS
OF EMOTIONS—THE THINKING COMPONENT

1. Describe some thoughts you had the last time you felt anxious.

2. Describe some thoughts you have had when you felt guilty.

3. Describe some thoughts you have had when you felt excited.

PART TWO: PHYSIOLOGICAL—HOW YOU FEEL IN YOUR BODY

Both positive and negative emotions are associated with physical sensations/feelings in the body. Any time you experience anxiety, you may notice stomach distress, sweaty palms, or an increase in heart rate. You may experience "butterflies" when you get excited, or a sense of heaviness and lack of energy when you feel sad. If you have ever been in danger (or had a panic attack), you may have noticed a fast-beating heart, shortness of breath, and lightheadedness. With anger, perhaps you felt your body temperature increase, your muscles tighten, and your heart pound. If you have paid attention to disgust, you may notice that you experience heart racing and pounding, nausea, and turning down the corners of your mouth. With shame, you may have experienced an increase in body temperature, sweating, and nausea symptoms. Remember, these physical sensations serve an adaptive purpose to protect you, not hurt you!

Many people who struggle with chronic anxiety have what we call *anxiety sensitivity*. Anxiety sensitivity occurs when the person with chronic anxiety is uncomfortable with the bodily sensations associated with anxiety and has the perception that these symptoms will have negative social consequences. Anxiety sensitivity has both a hereditary component, similar to neuroticism, and an environmental one. As noted in earlier chapters, the fall brought forth in many individuals a genetic predisposition toward negative emotionality. Some people are born with an overactive limbic system, which creates sensitivity to negative emotions and the situations in which these emotions may occur.[1] The limbic system is the part of the brain that is responsible for managing emotions, memory, and learning.[2] In the case of anxiety sensitivity, it involves the perception that the physical symptoms of anxiety are dangerous in addition to remembering the situations where these symptoms occurred.[3] Unfortunately, this tendency toward anxiety sensitivity is often modeled for children within the context of the family, and since children view the world through the lens of their caregiver, they often develop this same tendency.[4] (We will discuss ways to reprogram anxiety sensitivity in chapter eight, "Being Physical.")

REFLECTION: UNDERSTANDING THE PARTS OF EMOTIONS—THE PHYSICAL COMPONENT

1. Describe the feelings in your body when you've been anxious.

2. Describe the feelings you had in your body when you experienced sadness.

3. Describe the feelings in your body when you've been angry.

PART THREE: BEHAVIORAL—WHAT YOU DO

Every emotion includes an urge to act or respond to a given situation. We raise our hands or clap our hands during praise when we experience joy. Similarly, we slam on our breaks when there is a car accident ahead. Behaviors can also involve mental "acts" including praying, counting, and planning. However, we often engage in behaviors that don't seem particularly helpful during a given situation. For example, in response to shame, we may send a text message to someone who is upset with us instead of having a face-to-face conversation. In response to anxiety, we may avoid a church function where we could meet new people. Someone who feels sad or depressed may eat ice cream and watch Netflix instead of getting some sunshine and walking the dog. However, it would be normal for the same individual who experienced a recent ending of a relationship to temporarily withdraw from social interaction in order to process the memories from the relationship while not being interested in leisure activities for a season. In the first example, notice that eating and watching Netflix in response to sadness may initially feel good, but this response typically backfires and perpetuates more feelings of depression. In contrast, temporarily withdrawing from social interaction in order to process the memories from a relationship may initially feel bad but leads to new learning about relationships and a lessening of sadness.

Similarly, if you recently experienced a traumatic event that involved personal injury or harm, it would be normal to experience intense negative emotions when reminded of this event, and to attempt to avoid situations similar to where the event occurred. However, it would be an unhealthy response if you avoided all places or activities involving people based on anxiety about the potential of a traumatic event happening again. Think of some behaviors that you engaged in when you experienced strong emotion. Were they an appropriate level of intensity for the situation?

REFLECTION: UNDERSTANDING THE PARTS OF EMOTIONS—THE BEHAVIORAL COMPONENT

1. What did you do in a situation in which you felt anxious?

2. What did you do in a situation in which you felt sad?

3. What did you do in a situation in which you felt angry?

4. What did you do in a situation in which you experienced the joy of the Lord?

PUTTING IT ALL TOGETHER

Emotions serve an adaptive purpose and were designed to help us navigate the world around us. We often lose our way when we respond negatively to emotions, which leads us to engage in behaviors that may provide temporary relief but reinforce the negative emotions we are trying to manage. Spiritually, mastering your emotions allows you to protect your heart by lining up your soul with your spirit so that you can receive and experience the fullness of Jesus Christ in your life.

HOMEWORK

1. **Pray:** Ask the Holy Spirit to give you wisdom and revelation about which emotions have been the biggest hindrances to your walk with the Lord and within your relationships. Label and record three of those emotions below.

   A:

   B:

   C:

2. **Practice:** Identify the situation that triggers Emotion A this week and record it, as well as the three parts of Emotion A.

   - Emotion A situation/trigger:

   - Emotion A thoughts: What am I thinking?

   - Emotion A physical sensations: What am I feeling in my body?

   - Emotion A behaviors: What am I doing / do I feel like doing?

3. *Practice:* Identify the situation that triggers Emotion B this week and record it, as well as the three parts of Emotion B.

- Emotion B situation/trigger:

- Emotion B thoughts: What am I thinking?

- Emotion B physical sensations: What am I feeling in my body?

- Emotion B behaviors: What am I doing / do I feel like doing?

4. *Practice:* Identify the situation that triggers Emotion C this week and record it, as well as the three parts of Emotion C.

- Emotion C situation/trigger:

- Emotion C thoughts: What am I thinking?

- Emotion C physical sensations: What am I feeling in my body?

- Emotion C behaviors: What am I doing / do I feel like doing?

You can use the "Three Parts of an Emotion" worksheet to help you in identifying your triad of emotion in the upcoming week.

THE THREE PARTS OF AN EMOTION WORKSHEET

Describe the trigger:

What emotion(s) did you experience? (one word)

THOUGHTS
What am I thinking?

PHYSICAL SENSATIONS
What am I feeling in my body?

BEHAVIORS
What am I doing / what do I feel like doing?

4

BEING AN EMOTIONAL MASTER

KNOWING THE SEAL OF EMOTIONS

Keep your heart with all diligence,
For out of it spring the issues of life.

PROVERBS 4:23

In the previous two chapters, we learned about how some of us are predisposed to experience intense negative emotions (the emotional consequence for many after the fall), about the purpose of an emotion, and about the three parts of an emotion. We also learned that both positive and negative emotions are meant to help us pay attention to important things around us so that we can navigate our world successfully. In this chapter, we will address the importance of recognizing that all emotions occur within a context.

The Word of God tells us, "Keep your heart with all diligence, for out of it *spring* the issues of life" (Proverbs 4:23). Without understanding emotions in context, believers struggle to recognize situations that trigger negative emotions and the cycle of avoiding emotions, which backfires and contributes to the continuation of the same emotion. By protecting your heart with a

SEAL, you will be able to observe your emotions in context and simultaneously allow the Holy Spirit to direct you to respond to your environment adaptively.

UNDERSTANDING YOUR EMOTIONAL SEAL

Understanding your emotional SEAL is an easy way for you to learn to pay attention to your emotions as they occur in real time. SEAL is an acronym that explains this process by describing the *situation* that triggers your *emotions*, which then lead to consequences that occur right *afterward* and again *later on*.

S *refers to* **situation.** Your emotions always occur in a context and are triggered by events, both internal and external, even when it doesn't feel that way. For example, Sheila reports being devastated about her inability to attend church in person ever since she experienced a panic attack there. Though her first panic attack occurred at an aquarium, she recalls that the last time she attended church, she felt panicky due to feeling trapped. In fact, Sheila reports that she avoids any situation where escape might be difficult or embarrassing if she were to feel panicky, including shopping centers, movie theaters, traffic, and rooms without windows. In this example, the external situation that appears to trigger Sheila's panic is a place involving crowds or an enclosed place. External triggers always involve something in one's environment whereas internal triggers include internal events such as thoughts, physical arousal, or images. Some other internal or physical triggers could include how you feel after drinking a cup of coffee, standing up too fast, or feeling your heart skip. Other examples of external triggers or situations might include receiving negative feedback from a boss, receiving bad news about a loved one, or hearing about an increase in violent crimes in your area.

EMOTIONAL EXPERIENCE	TRIGGER
Anxiety	• Not hearing back from your teenager after texting about their whereabouts • Having to speak in front of others • Receiving an email to meet with your boss
Sadness/ depression	• Receiving bad news • Hearing certain songs • Losing a loved one
Fear	• Your home alarm system being triggered in the middle of the night • Seeing a fight • Hearing gunshots
Panic	• Feeling trapped • Uncomfortable physical sensations that happen "out of the blue" • Having too much caffeine
Anger	• Being cut off in traffic • Being criticized by a loved one
Disgust	• Seeing a foreign object in your food • Seeing something immoral on TV
Shame	• Someone expressing disappointment in your behavior

E *refers to your* emotions. In chapter three, we discussed how emotions have three parts: thoughts, physical feelings, and behaviors. As we just mentioned, both internal and external events can trigger your emotions. This is where we become skilled at labeling our emotions and putting them in the three-part model. For example, let's revisit our friend Sheila. If you remember, the situation that triggered her emotion was a place involving crowds (church) or a place that is enclosed. Sheila's emotion was fear (panic) and involved the three parts displayed in the Three Parts of an Emotion worksheet: her thoughts of danger led to uncomfortable feelings in her body, which led her to the behavior of escaping church in order to feel better.

A *refers to what happens* afterward. Your emotional response always has short-term (afterward) consequences. For example, if you avoid church because you feel anxious, you will most likely feel better immediately afterward because your anxiety has subsided temporarily. Another example is feeling better right after yelling at your son when he wasn't ready on time, because he quickly got ready and got in the car after you yelled at him. Feeling better in this case is the direct result of a decrease in the physiological arousal associated with anger after the behavior of yelling. However, as we mentioned in chapter one, how we respond to negative emotions is typically the issue rather than the emotion itself; we often respond to these emotions in ways that make us feel better afterward but make us feel worse later. Based on the previous example, though your son may have obeyed because you yelled at him in the moment, what happens as a result of your response to your anger later on? How might your yelling affect your relationship with your son?

L *refers to what happens* later on. Let's take a final look at Sheila. Sheila reports feeling better after she escaped her church building. However, once she asked herself the long-term consequence for avoiding church (what happened later on), she realized that escaping made her feel more anxious about going back in the future. Not to mention, she missed out on a great message and fellowship with other believers. As you can see, the problem is how we respond to negative emotions: we might feel better afterward, but we feel worse later on. Proverbs 4:7 tells us that "wisdom *is* the principal thing; *therefore* get wisdom. And in all your getting, get understanding." Knowing that your emotions have triggers is important, but "the principal thing" is understanding what triggers your emotions and that how you respond to them either makes emotions stronger or allows you to respond to events in a godly fashion. As we move forward, you are going to learn skills that will teach you how to strengthen your soul and respond to your emotions in a godly manner.

REFLECTION: UNDERSTANDING EMOTIONS—
YOUR EMOTIONAL SEAL

1. What emotions do you find are the most difficult to manage? Why?

2. List some situations that trigger the strong emotions mentioned in question one above.

3. Your Emotional SEAL: In one of the situations listed above, how have you responded to a negative emotion that led to feeling better afterward but led to feeling worse later on?

- The situation was:

- The emotion was:

- Physical feelings:

- Thoughts:

- Behaviors:

- I felt better afterward when . . .

- Later on I felt worse because . . .

4. What did you learn about yourself as it relates to the short-term (afterward) and long-term (later on) consequences?

HOMEWORK

1. **Read** Proverbs 29:11 and 16:32.

2. **Pray:** Ask the Holy Spirit to give you wisdom and revelation about which emotions you need to completely surrender to Jesus. Pray this as a part of your prayer time every day.

3. **Practice:** Use the Your Emotional SEAL worksheet to identify triggers to your emotions and the consequences of your emotional responses for at least one, but up to three, situations that occur this week.

   - Identify up to three situations that trigger a negative emotion this week.

   - Label the three parts of the emotion.

   - List the consequences: short term (afterward) and long term (later on) for each emotion.

Situation

Emotions

Name your emotion:

Thoughts:

Physical sensations:

Behaviors:

CONSEQUENCE

Later On

How might this response
make you feel worse?

CONSEQUENCE

Afterward

How might this response
make you feel better initially?

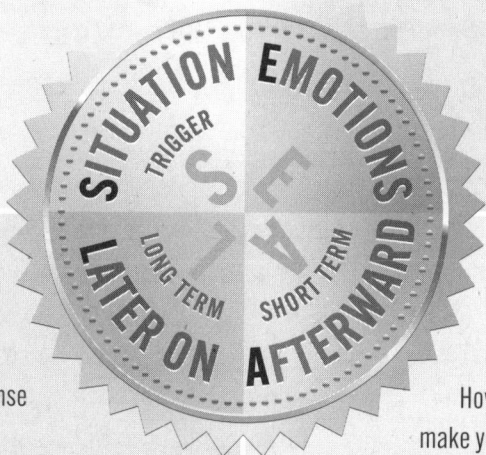

5

BEING PRESENT

You will show me the path of life;
In Your presence is fullness of joy.

PSALM 16:11

One of my favorite statements that I regularly say to clients is the following: "It is almost impossible to be in God's presence if you are not present." I have spoken to countless friends and clients about the difficulties they have with simply being present in the moment: present with their spouse, present when playing with their children, present while having a conversation, present while watching a movie, present during dinner, present during their prayer time, and present during worship. Having difficulties hearing God doesn't mean that he isn't speaking; in most cases, the noise of life is distracting you so that you are unable to focus your attention to the present. In the present, the most important moment in your life is this one, not the last one or the next one. In this chapter, you will learn one of the most important skills to help you manage your emotions, which is to be present and not judge your emotional experiences.

(NOT) JUDGING YOUR EMOTIONS

From the beginning, the devil's greatest trick has been deception. One of the most powerful ways that the devil tries to deceive you is by getting you to judge your emotions. Again, this same strategy occurred in the Garden of Eden and set the stage for many of us to experience negative emotions more than other people and to respond to these emotions in negative ways. You may be asking yourself, *What does he mean by judging my emotions?* Judging your emotions means either viewing your emotions as too intense to handle or believing that you shouldn't feel a certain way.

Along these lines, judging your emotions can be influenced by sin, particularly if you have a consistently dysregulated response to certain emotions. For example, if you were to struggle with pride and consistently perceive others as violating your concept of fairness, then you might respond to others with wrath because you feel the need to "give them a piece of your mind." In cases like this, judging your emotions by comparing them to what the Word of God says about these emotions would be prudent.

Additionally, judging your emotions could also be as simple as assuming a certain emotion is bad. For example, it is normal to get anxious about an upcoming speech, so judging this anxiety might be you saying to yourself, *I shouldn't feel this way. Why do I have to be so nervous?* Imagine what this judgment does to your anxiety; it makes it a lot worse and probably leads to more negative emotions.

Judging your emotions can also be in the form of telling yourself you should feel a certain way, such as assuming you should be experiencing more joy during praise at church or you should be more upset about what someone said about you. Again, judging your emotions leads to responding to them in a negative way. Imagine if Jesus had judged his anger in the temple. If Jesus had said, "I am too upset right now; I probably shouldn't drive them out of the temple since others might get the wrong impression of me," how might that story have changed? As previously noted, Jesus demonstrated righteous anger but also responded to his anger in a nonjudgmental fashion. His anger was justified, and his response was necessary.

BEING AWARE OF THE PRESENT

Equally important to not judging your emotions is becoming more aware of the present moment and responding to your emotions as they happen in real time. If you struggle with anxiety and worry, being present is probably extremely difficult since anxiety and worry involve future threat or danger. Being aware of the present moment is equally important for other emotions, including shame, guilt, sadness, frustration, and anger, and could prevent you from escaping or avoiding situations when these reactions are unnecessary. In other words, learning how to respond to what is happening right now is a skill that is necessary for not only enhancing your ability to fellowship with God (Psalm 16:11) but also for experiencing your emotions with less intensity.

In addition, being present will increase your experience with positive emotions. I was interviewed for Bloomberg Business Week on a phenomenon known as "the Smondays," which refers to people being anxious and upset on Sunday because they are thinking about all they have to do on Monday. The active skill of being present, along with expressing gratitude through prayer, will help you look forward to the work week (Craske et al., 2014, 10-23).[1] If we can take each moment in stride by focusing on the present moment, we will not get bogged down with negative emotions that have nothing to do with what is happening right now.

LEARNING HOW TO BE PRESENT

In order for us to be present, we must be mindful of what is currently happening and how to respond to it right now. So many

Christians struggle with hearing God in their everyday lives due to mental activity that often prevents them from simply being in the present with the Lord. Being present can be practiced in a number of ways, but I find the following ways the most helpful for believers: practicing when you aren't experiencing intense emotions, practicing by triggering an intense emotion on purpose, and practicing when someone or something triggers an intense emotion. These three ways of practicing will allow you to build the capacity of being present and draw you closer to God in the process.

EXERCISE 1: PIP—PRESENT IN HIS PRESENCE

The first skill is what I call PIP (Present in His Presence), which is directly linked to Psalm 16:11. As noted in Psalm 16:11, "In Your presence *is* fullness of joy." The PIP skill will assist you with posturing yourself to experience the joy of the Lord by intentionally being in his presence through "turning off" distractions and being present with him. I have created a script that allows you to practice the skill of turning off all distractions and simply meditating on Scripture while imagining yourself being in the presence of God. Practicing being PIP every day will help you build your "being present" muscles, and you will find it easier to rest in the presence of the Lord without distraction. The following PIP script is an example of a script that you may use as part of this exercise.

PIP SCRIPT

- Sit in a comfortable position with your back straight and your hands resting gently on your lap. Close your eyes and get settled in your seat. Take a deep breath, inhaling slowly through your nose and exhaling slowly out your mouth. As you exhale, release any tension or stress that may be present within you.

- Take a moment to anchor yourself in the present moment. Let go of all distractions and worries. Bring your attention to the here and now as you are sitting in this space.

- Psalm 46:10: "Be still, and know that I *am* God."

- Reflect on these words. Allow yourself to be still, both in body and in mind. In this stillness, find a sense of peace and surrender. Know that in this moment, you are connected to God, who is the source of all strength and wisdom. Let the stillness cover you.

- Continue inhaling slowly through your nose and exhaling slowly out your mouth.

- Isaiah 40:31: "But those who wait on the LORD shall renew *their* strength; they shall mount up with wings like eagles, they shall run and not be weary, they shall walk and not faint."

- Imagine yourself waiting patiently for the Lord, like an eagle perched on a mountain peak. Feel the strength welling up within you as you wait for the Lord to guide you. Visualize yourself soaring high, free from the burdens of weariness and doubt. Allow the promise of renewed strength to fill your soul.

- Inhale deeply, envisioning yourself soaring, and exhale any weariness or doubt.

- Philippians 4:6-7: "Be anxious for nothing, but in every-thing by prayer and supplication, with thanksgiving, let your requests be made known to God; and the peace of God, which surpasses all understanding, will guard your hearts and minds through Christ Jesus."

- Release any anxieties or worries that you may be carrying. Bring your concerns to Jesus with gratitude in your heart. Know that as you surrender your troubles, a profound peace, one that transcends understanding, covers you, guarding your heart and mind.

- Breathe deeply, releasing anxiety and accepting the peace that surrounds you.

- As you settle into this moment, bring your awareness to the words of the Scriptures that remind us of the presence of God in our lives.

- Psalm 16:11: "You will show me the path of life; in Your presence is fullness of joy; at Your right hand *are* pleasures forevermore."

- In this moment, reflect on being in the presence of God. There is fullness of joy in his presence. Remain present in the presence of God, who shows you the path of life. Imagine yourself walking this path, surrounded by joy and everlasting peace.

- Exodus 33:14: "My Presence will go *with you*, and I will give you rest."

- Feel the comforting presence of the Lord, offering rest and protection. The Lord's presence is with you in this moment, and he remains with you in any situation or circumstance.

- Deuteronomy 31:6: "Be strong and of good courage, do not fear nor be afraid of them; for the Lord your God, He *is* the One who goes with you. He will not leave you nor forsake you."

- Allow these words to reassure you that you are never alone, and that strength and courage are always available through the Lord's presence. The Lord will never leave you nor forsake you. Picture the Lord's presence with you as you are in this room.

- Psalm 46:10: "Be still, and know that I *am* God. I will be exalted among the nations, I will be exalted in the earth!"

- Take a moment to be still, to quiet your mind and know that

God is with you. Sense the exalted presence of the Lord all around you in time and space.

- Isaiah 43:2: "When you pass through the waters, I *will be* with you; and through the rivers, they shall not overflow you. When you walk through the fire, you shall not be burned, nor shall the flame scorch you."

- Visualize yourself walking through the challenges of life, knowing that God is with you, protecting and guiding you.

- John 10:27-28: "My sheep hear My voice, and I know them, and they follow Me. And I give them eternal life, and they shall never perish; neither shall anyone snatch them out of My hand."

- Imagine yourself as one of the sheep, hearing the comforting voice of the Divine and following in the path of eternal life and security. Stay here for a few moments. Picture yourself following the Lord as he calls you by name.

- Now take a few moments to sit in stillness, basking in the glory of the Lord's presence surrounding you, within you, and guiding your every step.

- When you are ready, picture yourself in this room and how you are coming into contact with the seat and the floor. Now, you may gently open your eyes. Amen.

ACTIVITY: PRACTICE BEING PIP

Read or create an audio recording of yourself or someone else reading the PIP script. You may practice this alone or with your group.

Practice being PIP, and discuss your ratings from the reflection section and why you gave it that rating.

REFLECTION: BEING PIP

1. What emotion(s) did you experience during the PIP exercise? Don't forget to put each emotion into its correct three parts.

Emotion:

Physical feelings:

Thoughts:

Behaviors:

2. On a scale from 0–10, with 10 being the most present, how present in his presence were you?

3. On a scale from 0–10, with 10 being not judging your emotions at all, how effective were you at allowing yourself to experience your emotions, without trying to push them away?

EXERCISE 2: WORSHIP MUSIC AND MOOD

Now that you have practiced allowing your emotions to happen without trying to push them away, and being PIP, it is time to practice being present by triggering an emotion on purpose. One of the most interesting and powerful ways to trigger an emotion is through music. Though worship music is meant to position us in our relationship with God to focus on how holy and worthy he is and how grateful we are for what he did for us through Jesus, many of us experience a number of different emotions due to the memories that we may associate with certain worship songs. Music is tied to our memories and memories are tied to our emotions. Any song of any genre that is associated with negative emotions and memories would work for this exercise. For some of you, it could just be that the chords of a particular song sound sad. For others, it may be that certain negative emotions are tied to specific songs. For example, a song that has triggered sadness for me in the past is "Good Good Father," not because I don't believe that God is a good Father but because we worshiped to this song at church shortly after we put our family dog down earlier that day.

Practice playing worship music once a day for the next week to a song that triggers an intense emotion. Remember, the purpose of this exercise is to allow yourself to experience an intense emotion while not trying to push it away, apologize for it, turn down the volume because of the intensity, or engage in any other subtle form of judging. Rate your emotional experience as well as how mindful of the present you were and how nonjudgmental or judgmental you were of the emotion. The key is allowing yourself to sit with whatever emotion arises and not pushing the emotion away. Riding the wave of the emotion will teach you how to build your tolerance for feeling uncomfortable, especially in future situations when emotions are triggered by real circumstances.

ACTIVITY: WORSHIP MUSIC AND MOOD

Pick one song from the list below (or another song of your choice), and listen to the song without talking.

- "Belovedness" by Sarah Kroger
- "Christmas Shoes" by NewSong
- "Out of Hiding" by Steffany Gretzinger

- "Two" by Sleeping At Last
- "The Father's Song" by Upperroom

REFLECTION: WORSHIP MUSIC AND MOOD

1. What emotion(s) did you experience during the Worship Music and Mood exercise? Don't forget to put each emotion into its correct three parts.

Emotion:

Physical feelings:

Thoughts:

Behaviors:

2. On a scale from 0–10, with 10 being the most present, how present were you?

3. On a scale from 0–10, with 10 being not judging your emotions at all, how effective were you at not judging your emotion(s)?

EXERCISE 3: PATIENT SOUL (PS)

By your patience possess your souls.

Luke 21:19

Possessing the soul is essential for a believer. Additionally, possessing your soul requires patience, a key manifestation of the fruit of the Spirit. Another way to think about possessing your soul is regulating your emotions on a regular basis. Regulating your emotions when they are triggered requires you to activate patience before responding to your emotions.

Further evidence of this process is found in James 1:19, which reads, "So then, my beloved brethren, let every man be swift to hear, slow to speak, slow to wrath." In order for you to effectively respond to both internal and external events, you have to initially "hear" what is happening before responding.

Regardless of the type of emotional experience, you must possess your soul by processing both internal and external information and then responding to what is happening. Furthermore, having a patient soul requires frequent intentional practice, even when strong emotions are not triggered. As reading the Bible on a consistent basis is necessary for a believer to recall Scriptures in key moments, practicing the Patient Soul skill requires the same consistency. The key to the PS skill is practice: you will not possess your patience effectively when you need to unless you practice when you don't need to. These simple steps should help you activate a patient soul in moments when you experience intense emotions.

Consider this example of practicing the PS skill. Imagine that you are at church on a Sunday morning and you're trying to concentrate during praise and worship. You notice that you are having a hard time being present because you are experiencing the "Smondays" as you think about all of the work you have to do for tomorrow. You decide to take action and use the PS skill. First, you begin by using 4-6 breathing to be in this moment. Second, you recall your emotional triad and identify yourself as having the following thought: *I have so much to get done after church. How can I do it all?* Your physical feelings consist of an upset stomach and tightness in your muscles. You engage in the following behaviors: looking at your watch and picturing yourself being unprepared for

THE PATIENT SOUL
Follow these three simple steps when a strong emotion occurs in real time.

1

4-6 Breathing
Inhale for 4 seconds through your nose; exhale for 6 seconds out your mouth.

2

My Triad
What am I thinking in this moment? What am I feeling in my body in this moment? What am I doing / do I feel like doing in this moment?

3

Patient Soul
Engage in an action that is important for the present moment.

the two meetings that you have in the morning. Third, you are able to remind yourself that there is nothing you can do in this moment about work and that what is important in this moment is focusing on how good God is to you and your family. You decide to pay attention to the words of the songs, then on taking notes during the message. You also decide that you will set aside some time after lunch to write down what you need to do for work tomorrow.

Remember, the PS skill requires practice and repetition. As such, it is important for you to practice this skill on a regular basis. I usually suggest practicing this skill twice per day whenever you want and as needed when intense emotions arise.

REFLECTION: PATIENT SOUL (PS)

Think about and record some situations where the Patient Soul skill will be helpful to you.

HOMEWORK

1. **Read** Psalm 4:4; 16:11; and James 1:19.

2. **Pray:** Ask the Holy Spirit to give you wisdom and revelation about what situations trigger intense emotions in you and to show you how to be slow to speak and slow to react. Ask him to show you how to respond in a godly manner to situations that have been difficult to manage in the past.

3. **Practice:**

   - Practice the Present in His Presence (PIP) skill once or twice daily.

   - Practice the Worship Music and Mood skill at least once this week.

   - Practice the Patient Soul skill twice a day, and use it when strong emotions are triggered.

6

BEING RENEWED

*And do not be conformed to this world, but be transformed
by the renewing of your mind, that you may prove what is
that good and acceptable and perfect will of God.*

ROMANS 12:2

earning to be renewed is a very important (and my favorite)
skill that allows you to partner with the Holy Spirit in re-
programing your tendency to overreact in situations with intense emotions. The Word of God tells us that through renewing
our minds, we can prove the good, acceptable, and perfect will
of God.

Interestingly, psychological science also supports the notion
that our thinking patterns are influenced by our interactions with
the world around us, which suggests that we can be conformed
to the world based on what we allow ourselves to consume in
the world.[1] At an early age we develop core beliefs, based on our
learning experiences with our family of origin/caregivers, in three
interrelated areas: thoughts about ourselves, thoughts about the
world, and thoughts about other people.[2]

As believers, our life experiences also influence our thoughts
about God. Along these lines, our core beliefs about ourselves, the

world, and others/God often sound as follows: "I am _____, the world is_____, and others are/God is _____." Over time, if we have a tendency toward negative emotionality, have negative life experiences, or receive negative messages from our family of origin, we often develop core beliefs that conflict with who we are according to the Bible. When this negative learning occurs, we might think about ourselves in a negative light, think of others as "more put together" or untrustworthy, and think about the future as dangerous. Our thoughts about God are also shaped by similar experiences, and we can unfortunately learn to view God as condemning, distant, or angry. In addition, we often learn to view negative emotions as dangerous and think that we are unable to cope with them.

The good news is that you can change the way you think if you practice. Changing your thought life is not as simple as just thinking positively; it is more important that you learn how to be renewed in your thinking. This requires asking yourself if there are other ways to view situations that will lead to different emotional experiences,[3] as well as studying the Bible and letting Scripture influence your thinking patterns.

Proverbs 23:7 states, "For as he thinks in his heart, so *is* he." If you have learned to think of yourself as not being a morning person, you will never be a morning person. If you think of yourself as type A, then you can't be anything else. If you think of yourself as a hothead, you will always respond to anger in a negative way. If you think of yourself as a "worry wart," then you will always respond to anxiety with worry. The good news is that both the Word of God and cognitive-behavioral therapy reveal the same truth: in order to change the way you think, you must initially be aware of these negative thoughts and then "think on" different thoughts. Along these lines, the method that I use with clients on a regular basis is to help them (1) identify the thoughts that lead to negative emotions, (2) identify the traps in the way they think about a given situation, (3) learn how to challenge their thoughts with truth (kingdom questions), and (4) replace these thoughts by "putting on" alternative thoughts.

"For as he thinks in his heart, so *is* he." PROVERBS 23:7		
Common Statements That Leave People Stuck in Negative Emotional Cycles		
"I'm type A"	"I'm a hothead"	"I'm not a people person"
"I'm a control freak"	"I'm an introvert"	"I'm lazy"
"My nerves are bad"	"I don't do crowds"	"I'm so ADD"
"I'm so OCD"	"I'm not a morning person"	"You know I'm stubborn"
"I'm a worry wart"	"I'm antisocial"	"I have no patience"

IDENTIFYING AUTOMATIC THOUGHTS (ATS) AND NEGATIVE AUTOMATIC THOUGHTS (NATS)

If you struggle with negative emotions on a regular basis, it is likely that you have learned to think in a way that feeds the negative emotions. Our past experiences influence how we think about current situations, which is usually not a bad thing. In fact, our past experience with a situation (or an emotion) helps us make sense of our world so that we can respond in a beneficial manner. For example, when I go to Chick-fil-A, I don't have to look at the menu to order because I know that a #2 combo meal is a spicy chicken deluxe sandwich (with fries and a lemonade of course). So, when I go to a Chick-fil-A restaurant, I can confidently order a #2 and know that it will be correct. My experience with the #2 combo meal helps me decide in the future about ordering my food. Over time, these thoughts happen automatically and become what we call automatic thoughts (ATs): thoughts that pop into our minds even when we are not intentionally thinking them.

However, our automatic thoughts can also be negative and lead to intense emotions, particularly when the situation does not call for these emotions. For example, if you struggle with social anxiety, you might recall the first experience that contributed to your current social anxiety. Some individuals report giving a speech in the past and thinking to themselves, *I am going to make a fool of myself*, or *They can see how nervous I am*. If this occurs, our limbic system is designed to remind us of "threat," and therefore, we attempt to avoid situations where this threat may occur.[4] We can then notice a pattern of thinking that includes negative automatic thoughts associated with anxiety about being judged in social situations when, in most cases, no one is paying attention to us.

Another example is being rejected by someone in the past and thinking to yourself, *No one will ever love me*. When this negative automatic thought is paired with intense emotions such as shame or sadness, a pattern of negative automatic thought emerges that negatively affects your current and future relationships. A similar pattern can occur if you contracted a virus by eating contaminated food (disgust), failed to meet a loved one's standard (guilt), or were taken advantage of by peers (anger).

Notice the deception that takes place with negative automatic thoughts: The initial experience from when I first noticed a negative automatic thought that led to an intense emotion is not what is maintaining my negative thoughts today. The avoidance of these situations and the lack of paying attention to thoughts associated with my victory in Jesus is. Can you see how automatic thoughts, if negative (NATs), can intensify negative emotions?

REFLECTION: NEGATIVE AUTOMATIC THOUGHTS

1. What are your first automatic thoughts (the first thoughts that come to mind) when you read the following text message or email from someone important to you? "Hey, I need to talk to you about something, let me know when you are available, thanks!" Record at least two automatic thoughts.

2. What emotions might you experience based on these automatic thoughts?

Keep in mind, ATs aren't wrong or bad. The issue with some
of them is that they restrict what emotions you are able to experience, especially because most people think the automatic
thoughts they have are absolutely true or a fact. For example, if
your automatic thought is *I'm going to fail this test*, and you believe
it is true when it may not be (the majority of automatic thoughts
are not actually facts), then your automatic thought only leads
to negative emotions. While not all ATs are negative and lead to
negative emotions, people who struggle with intense emotions
are more likely to have a component to their automatic thoughts
that causes emotions to feel stronger. This component is what
we call a thinking error. Thinking errors are what cause ATs to
seem as if they are facts when in reality they are not. Learning to
identify thinking errors will help you bring Proverbs 23:7 to life
and fulfill the destiny that God has for you.

IDENTIFYING THINKING ERRORS

Thinking errors occur when your automatic thoughts are a negative misinterpretation of what is happening in each situation.
Thinking errors are also described as cognitive distortions or
thinking traps. Put another way, thinking errors involve negative assumptions about a situation and the idea that it's impossible for there to be a positive outcome. When your automatic
thoughts have thinking errors, you are guaranteed to feel an intense emotion, making it hard to get out of an emotional rut.
Though there are a number of ways to classify thinking errors,

I find it best to simplify these thinking errors into two major categories: (1) jumping to conclusions and (2) magnification.

Jumping to conclusions. *Jumping to conclusions* is also known as *fortune telling* or *mind reading.* When you have an automatic thought in which you make a negative prediction about the future, you fall victim to this thinking error. For example, you are preparing to give a speech to a group of colleagues at work and think to yourself, *I am going to make a fool of myself.* This thinking error is an example of fortune telling. Though it is normal to experience anxiety about being prepared to present to a group, this thinking error will cause your anxiety to intensify and will likely lead to you feeling more upset than necessary. Even worse, it might lead you to shift your attention to your own thoughts, which will prevent you from presenting your content effectively to your colleagues.

When your automatic thought involves what people might think about you, the thinking error becomes mind reading. For example, let's say you wave at someone at the supermarket and they look away. You then say to yourself, *They clearly don't like me.* This is a thinking error because there could be other explanations as to why they looked away.

Common examples of jumping to conclusions include:

- "They are going to think I don't have enough experience."
- "I am not going to do well on this exam."
- "They will make fun of me for this."
- "She is going to be so upset with me."
- "I did something wrong."

Don't confuse feelings with facts: the problem with thinking errors is that they sound like facts and, therefore, restrict what emotions you are able to experience in each situation. There are a number of ways to view a situation, but thinking errors convince you that there is only one.

REFLECTION: JUMPING TO CONCLUSIONS

1. What emotion would you likely feel if you concluded, *They clearly don't like me*?

2. Describe a situation where you engaged in mind reading and what emotions this thinking error led to.

Magnification. *Magnification* is when you blow a problem out of proportion. We also call this thinking error *catastrophizing* and *minimization*, since you are not only blowing the situation out of proportion, but you are also minimizing your ability to cope with the situation.

Common examples of magnification include:

- "God can't use a dirty vessel."
- "This is the worst day of my life!"
- Using the words *always* and *never* to describe negative events, such as "This always happens to me" or "I never do this right."
- "I can't take this anymore!"
- "I will never find a job as good as my old one."
- "You are always jumping on my case!"
- "I can't handle another setback."

REFLECTION: MAGNIFICATION

1. Give an example of when you were guilty of magnification.

2. What emotion(s) did you experience when you engaged in magnification?

USING KINGDOM QUESTIONS

One of my favorite methods to use when helping clients be renewed is teaching them to ask kingdom questions that challenge their automatic thoughts with truth. Too often we say things to try to make our loved ones feel better by spoon-feeding them truth that they simply don't believe. For example, if your daughter says, "I'm the ugliest person in the world," you would naturally say, "No you're not," or "You are fearfully and wonderfully made." Have you noticed that statements like these rarely make people feel better? Why? Because their thoughts are based on how they are feeling, not on facts. This is one of the greatest tactics of the enemy: to try to convince us that we are not who God says we are and since we feel bad, things must be bad.

Rather than spoon-feeding your loved one, practice using kingdom questions instead. Here is an illustration of using kingdom questions that I practice with clients that involves football. Suppose a wide receiver catches the ball. They run past a defender and make it to the 40-yard line, the 35, the 30, the 20, the 10, and they get tackled as they fall into the end zone. The referee looks at where the player was tackled and then throws both hands in the air above his head. What's that called? If you are a football fan or have ever watched football, you're probably thinking, *That's a touchdown*. Notice I didn't tell you it was a touchdown (spoon-feeding); I led you in the right direction and asked you the right question to get you to see what I already knew.

Kingdom questions are designed to align your thinking with the truths of God's Word and the values contained in God's kingdom. Kingdom questions are not simply based on facts but are also based on biblical truths. Kingdom questions will encourage you to look at other possible outcomes if you practice using them on a regular basis. In doing so, your emotions will become significantly less intense, and you will feel more confident about your ability to manage them.

Below is a list of kingdom questions you can use to help challenge automatic thoughts. Pick your favorite ones and memorize them over time.

- What's the evidence that this thought is true?
- What does God's Word say about this outcome?
- Am I certain that this thought is true?
- Am I 100 percent sure that this negative outcome will occur?
- Do I have a crystal ball? Can I tell the future?
- Does _____ mean_____?
- What happened in the past?
- Even if this negative event does occur, can I cope with that?
- What does 2 Timothy 1:7 say about this situation?
- What is a Bible verse that contradicts this outcome?
- What fruit of the Spirit will help counter this thought?

PUTTING ON THE NEW ME

Ephesians 4:24 tells us to "put on the new man which was created according to God, in true righteousness and holiness." Putting on the "new man," also known as the "new me," that is contained in our spirit requires us to know the truth, which will make us free (John 8:32). It's not the truth that will make you free; but rather, it's the truth *that you know* that will make you free. In other words, the act of knowing the truth will make you free rather than the truth itself.

Once you have practiced using kingdom questions, the answers to your kingdom questions should lead you to truth that you have to "put on" by declaring it, especially in situations when you experience intense emotions. Use this Old Me / New Me dialogue to start fighting back.

For example, say you attend church and hear a great message on fulfilling God's purpose for your life, but you leave feeling discouraged. You may have several automatic thoughts but let's assume it's this one: *I will never fulfill my destiny.*

After learning the skills in this book, you start fighting back by using the Old Me / New Me dialogue:

Old Me: "I will never fulfill my destiny."

New Me: "What's the evidence that I will never fulfill my destiny?"

Old Me: "I don't feel like I know what God wants me to do."

New Me: "Does feeling like I don't know what God wants me to do mean I will never fulfill my destiny?"

Old Me: "No, but it would help to know what he wants me to do."

New Me: "What does God's Word say about this?"

Old Me: "That God has a good, acceptable, and perfect will for my life even if I don't know what it is."

New Me: "Do I have a crystal ball? Can I predict the future?"

Old Me: (laughs) "No."

New Me: "What is another explanation?"

Putting On the New Me: "God has a plan for my life, even if I don't know what it is right now. I will continue seeking him, knowing he is and always has been faithful."

If you practice using the Old Me / New Me dialogue, the intensity of your emotions will begin to decrease as you replace your thoughts with truth. In addition, you will be more confident in your ability to cope with uncomfortable situations.

It is often difficult to renew our minds with the Bible without identifying the thoughts that we have learned to think and the thinking errors that have added fuel to the fire. That is why the Old Me / New Me skill is so important and represents a major step in renewing your mind.

REFLECTION: BEING RENEWED

1. Think about what you have learned about automatic thoughts and thinking errors. What revelations have you had about yourself? Record these thoughts below.

2. What are some examples of negative automatic thoughts and thinking errors that you have fallen for? Record them in the chart below and, if you're completing this book with a group, discuss your examples with others.

NEGATIVE AUTOMATIC THOUGHT	THINKING ERROR
Example: "I will embarrass myself in front of the church."	Fortune telling

3. What are some upcoming situations where being renewed will be helpful to you? Record at least three.

1. *Read* Proverbs 23:7; Jeremiah 29:11; Romans 12:1-2; Ephesians 4:17-24; and 2 Timothy 1:7.

2. *Pray:* Ask the Holy Spirit to give you wisdom and revelation about what lies you have believed about yourself, others, and your future. Ask him to bring specific Scriptures to your remembrance that you can use to replace the lie when you find yourself experiencing an intense emotion. If you have a difficult time recalling Scripture, you may find an online concordance Bible helpful with this skill. Record at least three lies and truths (Scripture) that counter the lies.

Lie:

Truth:

Lie:

Truth:

Lie:

Truth:

3. *Practice:*

- Practice using the Old Me / New Me dialogue.
- Use the Being Renewed worksheet when you experience intense emotions this week.
- Memorize your favorite kingdom questions.

KINGDOM QUESTIONS WORKSHEET

Kingdom questions challenge automatic thoughts by helping you align your thinking with the truth's of God's Word and the values of God's kingdom. Pick your favorites, memorize them, or add additional questions that help you challenge automatic thoughts.

- What's the evidence that this thought is true?
- What does God's Word say about this outcome?
- Am I certain that this thought is true?
- Am I 100 percent sure that this negative outcome will occur?
- Do I have a crystal ball? Can I tell the future?
- Does _____ mean_____?
- What happened in the past?
- Even if this negative event does occur, can I cope with that?
- What does 2 Timothy 1:7 say about this situation?
- What is a Bible verse that contradicts this outcome?
- What fruit of the Spirit will help counter this thought?

Add additional kingdom questions of your own below:

THE OLD ME / NEW ME DIALOGUE WORKSHEET

Put on the new man.
EPHESIANS 4:24

OLD ME

NEW ME

OLD ME

NEW ME

OLD ME

NEW ME

OLD ME

NEW ME

OLD ME

NEW ME

OLD ME

NEW ME

OLD ME

NEW ME

OLD ME

NEW ME

PUTTING ON THE NEW ME

Use this worksheet to help you identify situations that require renewed thinking so that you can manage your emotions more effectively.

SITUATION / TRIGGER

NEGATIVE AUTOMATIC THOUGHTS

Kingdom questions are designed to align your thinking with the truths of God's Word and the values contained in God's kingdom. Ask yourself these questions to challenge automatic thoughts:

What's the evidence that this thought is true?

What does God's Word say about this outcome?

Am I 100 percent sure that this negative outcome will occur?

Do I have a crystal ball?

What is a Scripture that speaks against this?

Even if this negative event did occur, can I cope with it?

Does _____ mean _____? Could there be another explanation?

WHAT'S THE THINKING ERROR?

Use the Old Me / New Me dialogue to identify new thoughts.

OLD ME

NEW ME

PUTTING ON THE NEW ME

7

BEING ADAPTIVE

But be doers of the word, and not hearers only, deceiving yourselves.
For if anyone is a hearer of the word and not a doer, he is like a man
observing his natural face in a mirror; for he observes himself, goes
away, and immediately forgets what kind of man he was. But he
who looks into the perfect law of liberty and continues in it, and is
not a forgetful hearer but a doer of the work, this one will be blessed
in what he does.

JAMES 1:22-25

raditional cognitive theory would suggest that changing your thoughts is the key to emotional change (Beck 1995; Wright et al. 2017, 6-23).[1] This would be consistent with Romans 12:1-2 as noted in chapter six. However, decades of research literature would assert that behavioral change is equally important to changing thoughts. In fact, many of the most successful forms of therapy for emotional disorders often prioritize behavioral change prior to thought change due to its immediate impact on positive mood, the release of endorphins in the body (the natural, "feel good" hormones that are released when we move around), and the creation of new thoughts that lead to more action.[2] Furthermore, the Word of God gives us a number of examples linking thoughts to behaviors, both positively and negatively. Thoughts influence behaviors and behaviors influence thoughts. Thoughts influence physical sensations and vice versa; behaviors influence physical sensations and vice versa. The Bible tells us that sin is conceived in our hearts but is manifested through our actions.

One of the most important parts of your emotional experience that leads to emotional change is behavioral change. To be clear, I don't mean occasionally changing behaviors but rather intentionally responding differently to emotional situations on a regular basis. As a Christian, this requires you to intentionally be uncomfortable and become a doer of the Word and not a hearer only, as stated in James 1:22. Like most of the skills that we have discussed so far, being adaptive requires you to first identify what behaviors you are currently engaging in so you can learn how to change your behaviors.

Emotions naturally ebb and flow, with the intensity of emotions initially increasing, then eventually decreasing on their own. Too often, we don't believe we can handle the intensity of an emotion, so we never allow ourselves to learn that we can. I have had thousands of clients tell me when they have learned to confront emotions, it wasn't as bad as they thought it would be. I trust that you will learn this is true for you as well.

SWIFT TO HEAR, SLOW TO SPEAK

It is human nature to repeat what feels good in the moment and to avoid what feels bad. The problem with doing so is what we discussed in chapter three: we respond to situations with intense emotions in ways that often make us feel good in the short term (afterward) but make us feel worse in the long term (later on). For example, you may have "had enough" and gotten upset with a loved one by lashing out at them. When you lash out, this may lead to feeling better at first (short term) because you "gave them a piece of your mind." However, you usually feel worse once the smoke clears because lashing out likely damaged your relationship. Even worse, lashing out at someone because of anger usually leads to the same response the next time since it made you feel better temporarily.

You may be someone who gets nervous in social situations. In the short term, you have learned to sit alone and not speak to others. This makes you feel less nervous, but this ultimately backfires and leads to more anxiety the next time, not to mention that you may miss out on important social events, making new friends, or getting invited to places.

As we have previously discussed, our limbic system is activated when we feel threatened so that we may engage in specific behaviors that are important for survival (e.g., fight, flight, or freeze).[3] If we experience intense emotions in a given situation, regardless of if it is actually dangerous, our limbic system reminds us of our previous response by getting us to shift our attention to "threat," increasing our physical arousal, and leading to a behavioral response. Your body will respond to your dominant thought based on your learning history. Notice that the issue in these situations is not the emotion itself; the problem has more to do with how you have learned to respond to the emotions, which makes the emotions stronger long term. Being "swift to hear, slow to speak, slow to wrath" (James 1:19) is an important Scripture reference as it relates to our behavioral response in situations that trigger different emotions. Taking a step back in order to "listen" to your thoughts and allowing these thoughts to lead to an adaptive behavioral response is essential to mastering emotions. In other words, we must be swift to hear and slow to speak by paying attention to our current behaviors and learning more effective ways to respond to situations that trigger intense emotions.

What are some behaviors that you often engage in in response to emotions? Write them in the table below.

EMOTION	BEHAVIOR
Sometimes when I'm *anxious*, I ...	
Sometimes when I'm *angry*, I ...	
Sometimes when I'm *sad / depressed*, I ...	
Sometimes when I feel *guilty*, I ...	

EMOTIONAL AVOIDANCE

What is emotional avoidance? *Emotional avoidance* is defined as anything you do to try and make an emotion go away or become less intense. The problem with emotional avoidance is that we usually view the emotion (and the physical feelings that come with the emotion) as dangerous or threatening. Therefore, many people do everything possible to try to make the emotion go away or become less intense. How do you avoid emotions? Let's discuss five strategies many people use to avoid emotions: total avoidance, subtle avoidance, thought avoidance, safety signals, and emotional behaviors.

Total avoidance. The first type of emotional avoidance is easy to recognize; we refer to it as *total avoidance*. Total avoidance is completely avoiding a situation that triggers an intense emotion. When we engage in total avoidance, we often state, "I don't do _____" as if it is a part of who we are. These situations may include social gatherings, public speaking, crowds, theaters, driving on the interstate, leading a meeting, being assertive, open spaces, tunnels, bridges, apologizing, listening to certain songs, not being in the same space as someone who previously wronged you.

Subtle avoidance. *Subtle avoidance* refers to being in an uncomfortable situation but not fully experiencing the uncomfortable situation. I often refer to this as "I'm there, but I'm not completely there." For example, you may get anxious ordering food at a restaurant. Even though you order your food, you never make eye contact with the worker taking your order. Other examples include sitting alone in another room during family gatherings to avoid conversation, driving your car to social events "just in case" you get anxious and need to leave before your friend leaves, always using the self-checkout line at a supermarket to avoid people, not speaking to someone you don't like in a social setting, looking away during a sad scene in a movie, and always sitting in the aisle seat of a movie theater in case you believe you are in danger and "need" to escape.

Thought avoidance. Thought avoidance refers to things you do to keep your mind off uncomfortable thoughts. Examples include pushing away negative thoughts (which come back), distraction (video games, TV, music), or even taking a nap. One of the most common thought avoidance strategies that plagues many Christians is referred to as *worry*.

WORRY: A TYPE OF THOUGHT AVOIDANCE

> Therefore I say to you, do not worry about your life, what you will eat or what you will drink; nor about your body, what you will put on.
>
> Matthew 6:25

Worry is one of the most deceitful and misunderstood concepts for people, and Jesus himself tells us not to do it. One of the main reasons people struggle with worry is because they don't understand what it is. Let's briefly explore the process of worry.

First, most people confuse anxiety with worry when worry is always in response to the emotion of anxiety. In other words, worry and anxiety are not the same experiences. Rather, people use worry as an attempt to manage anxiety, but it never works. It should also be noted that anxiety and worry have a bidirectional relationship; anxious thoughts often lead to worry as an attempt to manage anxiety, but worry as a strategy leads to more anxiety in the future. Worry is defined as repetitive negative thoughts about possible negative outcomes in the future. Those negative thoughts are typically about the potential outcome to a given situation.

Second, notice what Jesus says about worry in Matthew 6:25; he tells us, "Therefore I say to you, do not worry." Right before verse 25, Jesus tells us that we cannot serve God and mammon (riches or material wealth). In other words, when we put our trust in the uncertainty of whether we will have our needs met rather than resting in our needs already being met through Jesus, worry is a natural response to this uncertainty. Additionally, worry tends to be focused on categories that most people think about on a regular basis, which are also addressed in Matthew 6. These "cares" or categories include our health, health of significant others, family, finances, work/school, and minor matters such as punctuality or small repairs. We begin to think about all the possible negative outcomes of these cares and think that we are somehow problem solving and preventing catastrophe from striking.

The reason worry is considered an avoidance strategy is because when we worry, we are avoiding both the emotions and the negative images of the feared outcome that is unlikely to happen to begin with. In other words, worry is a verbal-language process that occurs in our brains that shifts our attention away from "seeing" the images of the feared outcome and therefore prevents us from processing the emotions associated with the feared outcome.[4] For example, let's say you get anxious about an unknown physical sensation in your body. To cope with this anxiety, you decide to worry about the physical symptom. You begin checking "Dr. Google" for hours for what these symptoms might mean, asking your family members if these symptoms are normal, searching online for natural remedies for the pain, or distracting yourself. In the short term, you feel relief because it seems like you are problem solving. However, in the long term you are not solving anything, and it leads to more anxiety over time.

The difference between worry and problem solving is that problem solving leads to a final solution and a decrease in anxiety, whereas worry does not lead to a solution and increases anxiety over time. When we worry, we are often trying to reassure ourselves that the worst possible outcome will not happen. Ironically, checking "Dr. Google" regarding a physical ailment will usually lead to discovering the most feared possible outcome.

It is important to note that soul distress, in the form of worry, can be very uncomfortable and hard to manage for many of us. We can simultaneously recognize the importance of trust in the finished work of Jesus while acknowledging that our distress is real and uncomfortable. In Matthew 26:42, Jesus experienced distress in the garden of Gethsemane prior to his crucifixion, asking, "O My Father, if this cup cannot pass away from Me unless I drink it, Your will be done." The important takeaway of Jesus' prayer is that we will experience distress and discomfort but our focus needs to shift to surrender rather than symptoms. As believers, we need to rest in the certainty that we are healed by the stripes of Jesus as it says in 1 Peter 2:24, but know that if we face death, it is gain as Paul says in Philippians 1:21. In other words, although we will eventually experience physical death, we will ultimately experience eternal life, since we will spend eternity with Jesus where negative emotionality will no longer occur.

Finally, most people worry about events that have a very low probability of happening. Can you see how worry can deceive you by giving you the impression you are solving a problem that already has a low likelihood of happening to begin with? The concluding statement by Jesus in Matthew 6:33-34 ends with a very powerful antidote to worry: "But seek first the kingdom of God and His righteousness, and all these things shall be added to you. Therefore do not worry about tomorrow, for tomorrow will worry about its own things. Sufficient for the day *is* its own trouble." Remain in the present moment, be aware of the discomfort from worry, eliminate the strategy of worry, and acknowledge the necessity of trusting Jesus instead.

REFLECTION: WORRY VERSUS ANXIETY

1. **Read** Psalm 94:19; 139:23; and Proverbs 12:25. In your own words, how would you describe anxiety?

   Anxiety is:

2. **Read** Matthew 6:24-34 and Luke 12:22-34. In your own words, how would you describe worry?

   Worry is:

SAFETY SIGNALS

One of the most subtle avoidance strategies that you may use is what we call a *safety signal*. A safety signal is anything or anyone that you take with you to make you feel more comfortable in a situation that you perceive as dangerous. Safety signals work by reinforcing the idea that situations must be dangerous unless you have the object or person with you in the uncomfortable situation. In other words, many people condition themselves to manage

EXAMPLES OF EMOTIONAL AVOIDANCE

Total avoidance	Subtle avoidance	Thought avoidance	Safety signals	Emotional behaviors
Not going to crowded places	Not making eye contact when ordering food	Worry	Water bottle	Isolating in your room
Avoiding movie theaters	Not drinking caffeine to avoid the physical sensations	Changing the subject during a conversation	Your spouse	Watching Netflix
Not being home alone		Changing the channel	Carrying a smartphone	Eating junk food
Not driving on interstates	Wearing dark clothing to not stand out	Watching TV	A pet	Stonewalling your spouse, shutting down
			Taking unnecessary medications on trips	

intense emotions by carrying objects or taking certain people with them in situations that are not in fact dangerous, but "feel" dangerous. As a result, the limbic system is activated in these situations when the object or person is absent and, therefore, intense emotions occur.[5] Put another way, you learn to associate feeling less distressed when you have a safety signal with you, so it becomes habit to make sure you have it in uncomfortable situations.

To be clear, it is normal to have a support person with you in situations that are realistically challenging, such as awaiting news from a doctor or having to attend a parent-teacher conference. However, many people get so used to safety signals that they don't see them as a problem until they don't have the item with them. Some examples of safety signals of this type include water bottles, essential oils, cell phones, a bottle of medication, AirPods, and a "safe" person or pet. Though you feel prepared for anything in the short term with your safety signal, you may have the perception that you can't manage distress in the long term without your safety signal. In other words, safety signals allow you to avoid the intensity of emotions in the short term but keeping safety signals with you maintains the intensity of these emotions in the long term.

EMOTIONAL BEHAVIORS

Anything you do that is designed to decrease the intensity of an emotion is considered an *emotional behavior*. Emotional behaviors are driven by the emotion itself and often lead to feeling better in the short term and to negative consequences in the long term. For example, Steve lashes out at people who cut him off in traffic. Steve feels less angry in the short term because he "gave them a piece of his mind!" However, Steve learns to associate lashing out behavior with a decrease in anger intensity each time he feels angry, and he has damaged multiple relationships in doing so. Other emotional behaviors include binge eating when sad, isolating, drinking alcohol in excess, self-harm, using drugs, and seeking reassurance from other people when you think they are upset with you (which leads to them being annoyed). Now that you understand how emotional behaviors can feed negative emotions and make you feel stuck, let's talk about how to change these behaviors.

REFLECTION: EMOTIONAL AVOIDANCE

In the chart below, record three ways you avoid emotions and what happens afterward (short term) and later on (long term). Remember the five types of emotional avoidance are total avoidance, subtle avoidance, thought avoidance, safety signals, and emotional behaviors. Examples of each are in the previous chart titled Examples of Emotional Avoidance.

EMOTIONAL AVOIDANCE STRATEGY	AFTERWARD (SHORT TERM)	LATER ON (LONG TERM)
Example: Worry	Seemed like I was problem solving for the future	More anxious, problem was still there

REPLACING EMOTIONAL AVOIDANCE: IMITATING
CHRIST THROUGH ADAPTIVE BEHAVIORS

"Imitate me, just as I also *imitate* Christ" (1 Corinthians 11:1). The word "imitate" comes from the Greek verb *mimeomai* and means "to follow." Paul was speaking to fellow believers of the Corinthian church, urging them to engage in similar behaviors as he was, as he was engaging in similar behaviors as Jesus. In Ephesians 4:22, Paul further urged the Christians of the church at Ephesus to "put off, concerning your former conduct, the old man which grows corrupt according to the deceitful lusts." It is impossible to put off or put on any conduct (or behavior) without experiencing an emotion of some sort. This is reflected in the soul of the believer but requires understanding what you already have in your spirit, which includes all of the fruit of the Spirit found in Galatians 5:22. The fruit of the Spirit has nine manifestations that exemplify the characteristics of Jesus and exemplify our conduct toward God, our conduct toward others, and our self-conduct. By growing closer to the Lord and believing what the Word says about us in the Spirit, we can begin to manifest these characteristics accordingly.

Emotional behaviors can be thought of as habits, and these habits are often a part of the "old me." Much of the conduct of the old me was based on how we learned to react to situations around us. Now that we are born again and understand that emotional behaviors strengthen negative emotions, it makes sense to learn how to respond differently to the situations we are in, which also allows us to understand emotions better. We are usually aware that we are reacting in a negative fashion to situations but find ourselves doing so anyway and later saying, "I couldn't help it." Others are unaware of their emotional behaviors because they have become habits and may have been expected or accepted within our families of origin. In this case, we may not become aware of these emotional behaviors until we have consistent, corrective learning experiences through interacting with others who help us recognize that these behaviors are not healthy responses to our emotions. However, God has made a way for us to be victorious over emotions by equipping us with a new spirit that empowers us to imitate Christ.

It is human nature to repeat what feels good and to avoid what feels bad. We have now learned, however, that what feels good in the moment can make us feel way worse later (and lead to sin, which has its own natural consequences). For example, it makes some people feel much better to avoid talking to people at a party to decrease their anxiety (short term), but they feel worse when they leave the party because they may have missed opportunities to connect with new people and have increased their anxiety for the next party.

Adaptive behaviors represent a way of putting on Christ. The skill of being adaptive refers to any behaviors that allow you to experience the emotion you have been avoiding while allowing yourself to learn something new. Using the party example, rather than avoiding talking to people at the party, you could make the decision to talk to one person. Notice that you will more than likely still feel anxious at first (short term), but you will likely feel more confident and maybe gain a new friend (long term). If you typically lash out in response to anger, you could take a deep breath and state, "I need a minute," but return later (adaptive behavior). If you tend to withdraw when feeling sad, you could text someone or engage in a simple task while remaining in the presence of others (adaptive behaviors).

The key to engaging in an adaptive behavior is to understand that you will *still* experience the emotion that you typically avoid, but the intensity of the emotion will eventually go down by way of your brain disconnecting your typical emotional behavior from the emotion that you are trying to manage. The point of an adaptive behavior is not distraction but rather learning that you can tolerate feeling uncomfortable while training yourself to be swift to hear, slow to speak, and slow to wrath/emotional behaviors. Eventually, your brain will associate adaptive behaviors with your emotions, and your automatic response will reflect emotional mastery and, depending on the situation, fruit of the Spirit.

REFLECTION: ADAPTIVE BEHAVIORS

What are some examples of adaptive behaviors you can use to replace the emotional behaviors below?

Emotional behaviors	Adaptive behaviors
Constantly saying "I'm sorry" to others because you think you may have offended them	
Responding right away to a text message to not offend the person who sent it	
Not eating before a social event because you don't like the physical sensations that occur once at the event due to eating	
Pointing out something negative your spouse did because you are annoyed with him/her	

Remember, we are called to be doers of the Word, not hearers only. Though our habits often feel automatic, through the grace of God we can now take a step back, process the situation, and practice putting on the new me by changing our behaviors. What goes up (the physical sensation component of our emotions) must come down. Walking by faith is also changing a behavior that you don't "feel like" changing. However, walking by faith is also relying on the power of prayer, assembling ourselves with other believers to encourage us (Hebrews 10:25), and relying upon the Holy Spirit as our Helper to help us change unhelpful emotional patterns of responding. Be encouraged.

REFLECTION: ADAPTIVE ACTIONS

Record what you have learned about emotional avoidance and the behaviors you have learned that have kept you stuck in a rut.

HOMEWORK

1. **Read** Matthew 6:24-34; 1 Corinthians 11:1; Galatians 5:19-25; Ephesians 4:17-24; James 1:22-25; and 2:26.

2. **Pray:** Ask the Holy Spirit to give you wisdom and revelation about the ways you have avoided emotions and viewed emotions as dangerous. Ask him to guide you in using adaptive behaviors and paying attention to how he has seen you through uncomfortable or uncertain situations in the past.

3. *Practice:*

- Practice identifying the ways you have avoided emotions.
- Practice using the Emotional Behaviors worksheet to counter emotional avoidance.
- Revisit the other skills in this manual, especially chapters five and six.

IMITATING CHRIST WORKSHEET: Adaptive Behaviors

Record a situation you often avoid because it triggers an intense emotion. Identify the emotion(s) and write down the emotional behavior that you usually do. Next, write down your new adaptive behaviors.

SITUATION

EMOTIONS

EMOTIONAL BEHAVIORS

ADAPTIVE BEHAVIORS

8

BEING PHYSICAL

Therefore I run thus: not with uncertainty. Thus I fight: not as one who beats the air. But I discipline my body and bring it into subjection, lest, when I have preached to others, I myself should become disqualified.

1 CORINTHIANS 9:26-27

😆 😊 😲 😠

Though this Scripture is often used to describe the importance of being spiritually disciplined in order to be a good witness to others, I want to point out how this Scripture applies to you disciplining your body as you strengthen your soul. One aspect of disciplining your body is to not allow physical sensations to dictate how you respond in a given situation. To do so, strengthening your soul (particularly your mind) by renewing it to the Word of God and gaining knowledge is very important because it enables you to walk in the Spirit, which in turn allows you to discipline your body. Hosea 4:6 tells us that the lack of knowledge leads to destruction. This is true regarding the Word of God and can be true for other forms of knowledge that support the Word of God or God's creation. For example, in some cases, not understanding how God has designed our bodies to function can lead to a form of destruction in our lives. When we don't understand how God has created our bodies, we may misinterpret and/or overreact to what is happening inside of them, ultimately causing some sort of destruction, which is usually emotional.

BEING PHYSICAL: UNDERSTANDING THE NERVOUS SYSTEM

Having knowledge of your body's systems and the way God created them to function is crucial in managing the physical component of your emotional experience. One system in particular that is very beneficial to understand is the nervous system. Within the nervous system are two separate systems: the sympathetic nervous system and the parasympathetic nervous system. Both systems were created by God and are absolutely important for navigating our world. The sympathetic nervous system releases chemicals throughout your body to provide you with energy to take action. This is the "fight, flight, freeze" system.[1] The sympathetic nervous system is also involved with other emotional experiences, though the sensations may not feel as intense. For example, it is responsible for nausea when the emotion of disgust is triggered. Similarly, the sympathetic nervous system often remains continuously activated in conditions like depression, which creates a lack of energy, feelings of heaviness, and sleep disturbance. Furthermore, the sympathetic nervous system is indicated in negative emotions such as shame, guilt, anger, fear, anxiety, and disgust.

On the other hand, the parasympathetic (think "for sympathy") nervous system is the part of your nervous system that restores your body and returns it back to normal. It's important to understand that the parasympathetic nervous system always kicks in, even if you perceive the feelings of intense arousal as lasting forever. In other words, there is a tipping point for your arousal: intense physical sensations always come down despite the level of intensity. Furthermore, the parasympathetic nervous system is designed to prevent the sympathetic nervous system from going "too far," meaning this arousal is never dangerous. In the case of chronic sadness (depression), the parasympathetic nervous system does not become activated as quickly as it does with anxiety and fear.[2] It is also normal to experience a "hangover" effect once your parasympathetic nervous system kicks in. This is because the chemicals in your body that are triggered when the sympathetic nervous system is activated take some time to be eliminated from your system.[3]

Knowing that God designed our bodies with a parasympathetic nervous system and that intense arousal always has to eventually come down should be comforting for those who believe that there is no end to their distress. As you practice the being renewed skill from chapter six, saying to yourself "this too shall pass" would be a helpful statement to make in response to intense arousal.

It is important to note that the sympathetic nervous system is usually an all-or-nothing system, meaning that your body's organs are "full steam ahead" when in an activated state. For example, if you are in danger, your body is designed to prepare you to act by increasing blood flow to your core (the most important part of your body to fight or to run away), which may intensify heart palpitations. Other sensations that may occur in response to your body preparing you to fight, flight, or freeze include:

- Racing heart
- Shortness of breath
- Sweating
- Lightheadedness/dizziness
- Hot or cold flashes
- Tingling in hands and/or feet
- Chest tightness
- Nausea

- Derealization (feeling as if things around you are not real)
- Depersonalization (feeling that you are having an out of body experience)

Less intense symptoms that occur with other emotions that are triggered by the sympathetic nervous system include:

- Fatigue
- Lack of energy
- Heaviness in arms and legs
- Restlessness
- Difficulty concentrating or mind going blank

These sensations are important for survival in dangerous situations even though they may feel uncomfortable. However, what happens if we experience these sensations in situations that are *not* dangerous or when we have not done any physical activity to cause them (such as exercising)? As previously noted, when this occurs, people often say that the sensations came "out of the blue," and they associate the sensations they experienced with the situation or context they were in. For example, if you become lightheaded, have a hot flash, and your heart starts racing and pounding in church, you may interpret church as a dangerous place because you felt like you were going to pass out or have a heart attack there. In reality, church is not a dangerous environment and not what caused the sensations; you just happened to be in church when the sensations occurred. Because you have associated church with the sensations and deemed church as a dangerous place, you may now avoid it, which leads to more negative emotions, condemnation, etc.

If you were in actual danger, the sensations mentioned above all serve to protect you. For example, if you were being chased by a wild animal, blood would begin to flow to the parts of your body that need it most (large muscles) and away from the parts of your body that don't need it. This may cause you to feel as if your heart is beating out of your chest, may lead to lightheadedness, and you may also experience tingling in your hands and feet. Feeling as if you can't get a full breath (a common symptom of a panic attack) occurs when you are in danger because oxygen is flowing to the tissues in your large muscles to help you fight or flee. Sweating often occurs in dangerous situations to cool your body so that you don't overheat. Your stomach may "hurt" because your digestion is slowing down to prepare your body to pay attention to danger rather than food.[4] In other words, God equipped your body to deal with threat and danger by increasing activity in your sympathetic nervous system.

As noted earlier, your body is equipped for "checks and balances." Your parasympathetic nervous system *always* keeps your sympathetic nervous system in check and doesn't allow it to make your body feel activated for long, especially when danger passes. Ironically, no one pays attention to these sensations when in danger; we only seem to pay attention to them when they happen "out of the blue," such is when you may have had a panic attack in church. As you have learned, though panic attacks never happen out of the blue (they just feel that way sometimes), many people continue to struggle with the physical sensations that are part of their emotions because they associate these sensations with danger. Now that we have exposed this lie, let's talk about how to "be physical."

REFLECTION: THE PHYSICAL SYSTEM

1. What are some physical sensations you are sensitive to?

2. How did you learn to become sensitive to these physical sensations? (Where were you, what were you doing, and when did these events occur?)

3. What activities have you avoided because you are sensitive to certain physical sensations?

4. In the chart below, list some physical sensations you are sensitive to as well as some foods or activities that trigger these same physical sensations.

PHYSICAL SENSATIONS	ACTIVITIES
Example: Fast beating heart, stomach distress	Drinking caffeine, working out

You may have learned to view these normal physical sensations as dangerous due to negative events that have happened in your past in which you experienced anxiety, shame, sadness, anger, guilt, disgust, or fear. Such events may include negative social situations, traumatic events, loss of a loved one, being wronged by others, letting someone down, or being sick. This may cause you to associate current physical sensations that remind you of the past negative event with that event. It is important to remember, however, that though these sensations can be uncomfortable, they are all normal, necessary at times, and you can learn to tolerate them. Additionally, because they are part of the emotions you will regularly experience, it is necessary to confront them so that you no longer associate them with danger or threat. This is the key to being physical: confronting the physical sensations, learning they are not dangerous or threatening, and understanding that you can deal with intense emotions. In other words, it is time to increase your tolerance of being uncomfortable.

BEING PHYSICAL

Below is a list of exercises that I commonly use with clients to get them used to feeling the physical sensations that are a part of their emotional experiences. The being physical skill is *learning* that you can tolerate feeling these sensations and that your body will naturally calm itself down. This skill will help you approach, rather than avoid, activities that trigger intense emotions, as well as increase your tolerance of these emotions. (If you are concerned as to whether you are able to engage in some of these exercises due to a general medical condition, it is advised that you seek guidance from a physician.)

The following exercises are meant to mimic common physical sensations that you may experience when having an intense emotion. With these exercises, remember the key is identifying which exercises are the most uncomfortable for you and the

PHYSICAL SENSATION EXPERIMENT

Symptom experiment	Physical sensations	Distress level (0-10)	Familiarity (0-10)
Hyperventilate Rapidly inhale and exhale out your mouth for one minute			
Breathe through coffee stirrer Hold your nose and breathe normally through stirrer for one minute			
Run in place Rapidly run in place, with high knees if possible, for one minute			
Raise head quickly Place head between legs for one minute and then raise it quickly after the timer sounds			
Mirror stare Stare into your eyes in a mirror for one minute, resist distraction			
Tense muscles in body in front of a space heater Toes, feet, legs, stomach, chest, arms, shoulder, neck			
Spiral stare Find a video clip of a spinning spiral online and stare at it for one minute			

most similar to your emotional experiences. Once you identify which exercises are the most uncomfortable and familiar, your homework will involve you "being physical" by repeating these exercises for five minutes per day so that you can get used to these uncomfortable but normal physical sensations. Use the table above to complete your physical sensation test. If you are working in a small group, practice these exercises together. Do each of the exercises for one minute. After one minute, write down the sensations you experienced and provide a rating for both distress (how uncomfortable they made you) and familiarity (how familiar these sensations are to intense emotional experiences that you have). Higher numbers indicate higher distress and familiarity.

REFLECTION: BEING PHYSICAL

1. Use the table above to identify the physical sensations that trigger intense emotions.

2. Which physical sensation experiments were the most uncomfortable? Why?

3. Use the table below to describe which exercises stimulated physical sensations linked to intense emotions that you have struggled with.

PHYSICAL SENSATION EXPERIMENT	PHYSICAL SENSATIONS	WHAT EMOTIONS HAVE THESE SENSATIONS?
Example: Hyperventilation	Heart racing, shortness of breath, chest tightness	Fear, panic, anxiety

PHYSICAL SENSATION EXPERIMENT	PHYSICAL SENSATIONS	WHAT EMOTIONS HAVE THESE SENSATIONS?

Now that you have become familiar with the physical sensations that are a part of your emotional experiences, it's time to be even more physical. It is important that you do the exercises that are the most uncomfortable and familiar to you so that you can learn to master your emotions by way of mastering the physical sensations associated with your emotions.

HOMEWORK

1. **Read** Isaiah 40:29; 1 Corinthians 9:26-27; 2 Corinthians 4:17; Ephesians 6:10; Philippians 4:13; and 2 Timothy 1:7.

2. **Pray:** Ask the Holy Spirit to give you wisdom and revelation regarding activities or things you have avoided because you have viewed the physical sensations you have associated with these activities or things as threatening or dangerous. Ask him to guide you in confronting these sensations so that you can submit your body and master your emotions.

3. **Practice:**
   - Practice being physical by using the Being Physical at Home worksheet at the end of the chapter this week. Follow the instructions carefully.
   - Practice at least one activity that stimulates strong physical sensations this week, but complete as many exercises as are relevant to your emotional experiences.
   - Revisit the other skills in this chapter at your leisure.

THE BEING PHYSICAL AT HOME WORKSHEET

This worksheet is designed to help you identify what physical sensations you have struggled with and how to master these sensations. For at least one week, practice one exercise per day, doing each exercise five to seven times (trials) in a row. Label the exercise and rate your distress on a scale from 0-10 (with 10 meaning significant distress) after completing each trial.

EXERCISE

TRIAL / DAY   **DISTRESS LEVEL**

	1	2	3	4	5	6	7	8	9	10
1	○	○	○	○	○	○	○	○	○	○
2	○	○	○	○	○	○	○	○	○	○
3	○	○	○	○	○	○	○	○	○	○
4	○	○	○	○	○	○	○	○	○	○
5	○	○	○	○	○	○	○	○	○	○
6	○	○	○	○	○	○	○	○	○	○
7	○	○	○	○	○	○	○	○	○	○

EXERCISE

TRIAL / DAY   **DISTRESS LEVEL**

	1	2	3	4	5	6	7	8	9	10
1	○	○	○	○	○	○	○	○	○	○
2	○	○	○	○	○	○	○	○	○	○
3	○	○	○	○	○	○	○	○	○	○
4	○	○	○	○	○	○	○	○	○	○
5	○	○	○	○	○	○	○	○	○	○
6	○	○	○	○	○	○	○	○	○	○
7	○	○	○	○	○	○	○	○	○	○

EXERCISE

TRIAL / DAY   **DISTRESS LEVEL**

	1	2	3	4	5	6	7	8	9	10
1	○	○	○	○	○	○	○	○	○	○
2	○	○	○	○	○	○	○	○	○	○
3	○	○	○	○	○	○	○	○	○	○
4	○	○	○	○	○	○	○	○	○	○
5	○	○	○	○	○	○	○	○	○	○
6	○	○	○	○	○	○	○	○	○	○
7	○	○	○	○	○	○	○	○	○	○

9

BEING BRAVE

Finally, my brethren, be strong in the Lord and in the power
of His might. Put on the whole armor of God, that you
may be able to stand against the wiles of the devil.

EPHESIANS 6:10-11

God has equipped us with his whole armor. However, his armor is useless if we don't wear it. As Ephesians emphasizes the importance of putting on the Word of God as armor to combat spiritual forces of evil, this manual is designed to equip you with skills to master your emotions while partnering with God's Word to do so. Specifically, this manual has equipped you with the following skills: understanding where the tendency to experience intense emotions began, understanding the adaptive nature of emotions, recognizing the importance of understanding triggers and the consequences of your emotional responses, how to be present (patient soul), the importance of being renewed (the new me), the importance of being adaptive (engaging in adaptive behavioral actions), and the importance of being physical (tolerating physical sensations). It is now time to put on your full armor and learn how to take this wisdom and "get understanding" (Proverbs 4:7).

PREPARING TO CONFRONT EMOTIONS: BEING BRAVE

In order for the skills you have learned to be effective, you now have to, as James 1:22 states, "be doers of the word, and not hearers only." Just like we must "do," or practice the Word of God, we need to "do" or put into practice the knowledge we have gained from this manual. James 1:25 goes on to say, "But he who looks into the perfect law of liberty and continues *in it*, and is not a forgetful hearer but a doer of the work, this one will be blessed in what he does."

As a believer, being brave requires you to look into and continue in the "perfect law of liberty," which is the Word of God. Doing so leads to the freedom that is found in the Word of God. Reminding yourself of who you are in Christ, how much he loves you, and what he did for you helps to free you from being controlled by emotions and the situations in which they occur.

This passage in James also tells us to be doers of the "work" and that we will be blessed. Confronting emotions requires hard work and effort but leads to freedom and victory. You have been given effective skills that are confirmed by the Word of God.

Therefore, it is time to create a game plan so that you can combine your new skills into one piece of armor. For you to learn that you can tolerate intense emotions, you have to be willing to engage these emotions and the situations that trigger them until a new, nonthreatening association is created. Basically, you must "ride the wave" of the emotions so that you can learn (1) to tolerate intense emotions, (2) that the intensity of the emotions can't last forever, and (3) that these emotions will not hurt you. Living a life that is not dictated by feelings will undoubtedly enhance your relationships with God and those he has placed in your life.

It is critically important to remember that being brave will require you to confront situations multiple times to eliminate your negative response to emotions and learn that you can in fact tolerate intense emotions. Mastering emotions does not occur overnight. It is essential that you extend grace to yourself and remind yourself that emotions naturally ebb and flow. Similarly, remind yourself that repetition is necessary for a variety of skills that you have learned and emotional mastery is no exception. Any intense emotion you experience is temporary and by being brave (confronting these emotions multiple times), you will teach yourself that your body and your soul can be subject to your spirit and that you no longer have to let your emotions control your existence.

It is also important to note that many people reading this manual have struggled with emotional disorders and intense emotionality for a considerable amount of time, despite relying on God's Word for guidance in these areas. As a mental health professional, I highly recommend in these cases that you consider seeking additional counsel from a qualified mental health professional who can help you navigate the emotional difficulties that you have been experiencing.

BEING BRAVE: THREE TYPES OF EMOTIONAL EXPOSURE

The process of confronting situations that trigger emotions is what we call *exposure*. You are exposing yourself to both the situation and the emotions that are triggered by the situation until a new, nonthreatening association occurs. The length of time you spend confronting situations that trigger intense emotions depends on what you need to learn about the emotion and the situation in which it occurs.

Situational exposure. *Situational exposure* refers to being brave in situations that trigger strong emotions. Examples include crowded places, being assertive, eating a food that you have associated with sickness, going to a gravesite, looking at old photographs that you have avoided, asking an old friend out to lunch, driving or walking across bridges, public-speaking situations, meeting someone new, small talk, long lines, interstates, and being home alone.

REFLECTION: SITUATIONAL EXPOSURE

Brainstorm some situations that trigger strong emotions that you would like to conquer by being brave, and record them below.

Imaginal exposure. Imaginal exposure involves "imaging" (or imagining) a situation that triggers strong emotions. Imaginal exposure is particularly helpful for situations that are difficult to confront multiple times or have occurred in the past. Examples include dealing with past negative events, such as flying in an airplane, past embarrassment, and confronting worries. Imaginal exposure is also useful when people assume that thoughts about events are powerful enough to trigger a strong emotion. It is important to note that imaginal exposure is intended to trigger intense emotions on purpose so that you can tolerate being uncomfortable while learning a new, nonthreatening association.

The length of time that you engage in imaginal exposure depends on what you need to learn from the imaginal exposure. Asking yourself, *How will this exposure affect me, and can I tolerate the emotions?* prior to engaging in imaginal exposure will be helpful in understanding the purpose it serves. For example, will you not be able to enjoy your meal afterward if you think about a past embarrassment for twenty minutes? Will you not enjoy the movie with your spouse following thirty minutes of thinking about a sad time in your life? Will thinking about flying on an airplane for twenty-five minutes lead to you having a panic attack and not being able to complete tasks at work?

Imaginal exposure is an essential ingredient to treating severe trauma memories, as in the case of PTSD. If you have experienced significantly traumatic events that involved something that was life-threatening or similar in trauma intensity, it is highly recommended that you seek guidance from a mental health professional before proceeding with imaginal exposure.

REFLECTION: IMAGINAL EXPOSURE

Brainstorm some imaginal situations that trigger strong emotions that you would like to conquer through being brave, and record them below.

Physical sensation exposure. *Physical sensation exposure* involves confronting the physical sensations that are a part of intense emotional experiences and the stimuli that trigger these sensations. Think about the exercises from chapter eight and how many of these sensations and the activities that trigger them can bring on strong emotions, such as emotions triggered by hiking on a hot day, drinking caffeine, exercise, having a full stomach, sitting in a sauna, or raising your head quickly.

Adding physical sensation exposure to situational and imaginal exposure is a powerful way to master your emotions and is highly encouraged. Combining different types of triggers to emotional distress is known to enhance new learning, improve distress tolerance, and decrease sensitivity to intense emotions. Common examples of physical sensation exposure include running in place in the bathroom prior to ordering your food (being out of breath and talking to someone) and breathing through a coffee stirrer and then driving on the interstate (experiencing intense arousal while driving).

REFLECTION: PHYSICAL SENSATION EXPOSURE

Brainstorm some situations that trigger strong physical sensations that you would like to conquer through being brave, and record them below.

BEING BRAVE: CREATING YOUR MENU OF DISCOMFORT

Being brave by confronting situations that trigger strong emotions requires what is described in 1 Peter 5:8: "Be sober, be vigilant; because your adversary the devil walks about like a roaring lion, seeking whom he may devour." Being "sober" refers to thinking clearly, whereas being "vigilant" refers to being watchful. The reason these two concepts are so important is because they acknowledge that victory requires preparation: in order to adequately prepare for battle, you must have a plan that requires clear thought and attention to the right things. Confronting intense emotions and the situations in which they occur requires the same mentality. Therefore, having a structured plan for confronting situations that trigger intense emotions is extremely important for a number of reasons. First, it gives you a sense of mastery and control over the situations that trigger intense emotions. Second, it allows you to prepare in advance for uncomfortable situations instead of "winging it," which most people do when trying to manage emotions. Third, it allows you to pay attention to accurate information in the situations where intense emotions occur. Finally, it forces you to be objective: you will be able to think through the situations that trigger intense emotions like an outsider as you write the situations down on paper rather than remaining in your own head.

MY MENU OF DISCOMFORT WORKSHEET

SITUATION	DISCOMFORT (0-10)	AVOIDANCE (0-10)

Use the My Menu of Discomfort worksheet to structure to prepare for being brave. Write down the uncomfortable situation that you would like to master in the situation column. Using a scale from 0–10, with 0 indicating "no discomfort" and 10 indicating "extreme discomfort," rate each of these situations by level of distress. Finally, provide an avoidance rating for each of these situations in the avoidance column with 0 indicating "no avoidance" and 10 indicating "total avoidance." Though the order in which you confront these situations is not critical, I find it most helpful to begin with a situation that is rated a 3 for distress in order to build confidence and to increase the likelihood of success.

THE BEING BRAVE WORKSHEET

Now it's time to use the Being Brave worksheet at the end of this chapter to confront the situations that trigger intense emotions. There are several things to remember as you prepare for being brave.

1. ***Practice leads to mastery.*** It is important that you confront the situations on your menu multiple times throughout the week. I usually tell clients to engage in three to five "trials," or brave moments, per week. The more you practice, the more confidence you will gain in mastering your emotions.

2. ***Don't be discouraged.*** No one is perfect. Confronting emotions doesn't always go as planned. You may find that you confront something that is more intense than you expected, and therefore, you feel as if you failed at being brave. The enemy will use these "setbacks" as a way to bully you and to get you to pay attention to the problem and not the solution. You are more than a conqueror, and you do have power, love, and a sound mind. Exposure takes practice. If you fall off a surfboard, get back on the surfboard, pay attention to what you learned, and ride the wave of your emotions the next time. This too shall pass. Remember the emotional law of gravity. What goes up, must come down.

3. *Do not avoid!* This is arguably one of the most important points as you prepare for being brave: any form of avoidance will reinforce the intensity of the emotion and convince you that you cannot tolerate being uncomfortable. Although this is not true, many people live their entire lives believing this lie.

4. *Change the context.* It is important to change the context as you confront intense emotions. For example, if you struggle with social anxiety, you may get more comfortable ordering food at a certain restaurant in the presence of others, but what if you are faced with a different restaurant that has a different menu and you're by yourself? For your emotional learning to stick, it will be necessary for you to change as much as you can each time you confront each situation. This may include being alone, being tired, having others with you, time of day, being assertive with a different person, what interstate you confront, or if you have caffeine. Your brain needs to learn that it doesn't matter what the situation is. You are able to manage emotions regardless of the context.

REFLECTION: REVIEWING YOUR MENU

If you are completing your menu in a church fellowship group (such as a discipleship group, topical study group, Bible study group, small group, or life group) or other group format, please take this time to go over your exposure scenarios with others. Welcome feedback from those who you trust about discomfort ratings, avoidance ratings, items that you may need for your being brave exposures, and creative ways to confront intense emotions. Also take this time to identify someone to help you with accountability in completing your list of uncomfortable situations, preferably someone who is familiar with this book. As Proverbs 27:17 states, "Iron sharpens iron," so having weekly meetings, communicating by text messages, and engaging in phone calls will enhance your understanding of emotions and improve your relationships.

1. What negative automatic thoughts (NATs) will you need to identify as you prepare for being brave?

2. What emotional behaviors will you need to counter with adaptive behaviors as you prepare for being brave?

3. What physical sensations will you need to confront as you prepare for being brave?

4. In what ways can you combine different exposure exercises in order to challenge yourself while "killing two birds with one stone"?

1. **Read** Deuteronomy 31:8; Romans 8:36-39; 2 Timothy 1:7; James 1:22-25; 1 Peter 5:8; and 1 John 4:17-19.

2. **Pray:** "Holy Spirit, I thank you for being with me each step of the way as I confront emotions that are not meant to control me. I am not created to be controlled by my emotions; I am created to use my emotions to glorify God and to build his kingdom. Holy Spirit, give me wisdom, revelation, and creativity about how to confront situations that trigger intense emotions. I thank you for creating me to be brave as I renew my mind and walk in fullness. Thank you for making me aware of adaptive behaviors, how to be present, how to navigate physical sensations, and how to be flexible. I am strong in you and ready to be brave."

3. **Practice:**

   • Practice confronting the situations on your menu three to five times a week; make sure you change the settings as much as you can each time you confront the situations.

   • Revisit the other skills in this manual at your leisure.

   • Check in with an accountability person at least twice per week.

THE BEING BRAVE WORKSHEET:
Confronting Situations That Trigger Intense Emotions

DATE

BRAVE SITUATION
Describe the situation that triggers a strong emotion.

BEFORE THE SITUATION

Negative thoughts. What are the negative thoughts you may have about this situation?

Put on the new me. How can you think about this differently?

Adaptive behaviors. What behaviors will you choose rather than avoiding difficult emotions?

Be present. Remember: God will never leave you nor forsake you.

AFTER BEING BRAVE
What did you learn? For example, did you learn that you can tolerate being uncomfortable?
That the situation was not as bad as you thought it would be?
That your predicted outcome did not occur?

10

BEING CONSISTENT

Love has been perfected among us in this: that we may have boldness in the day of judgment; because as He is, so are we in this world. There is no fear in love; but perfect love casts out fear, because fear involves torment. But he who fears has not been made perfect in love. We love Him because He first loved us.

1 JOHN 4:17-19

As a believer, understanding what is stated in 1 John 4:17, "as He is, so are we in this world," is a powerful revelation, speaking to our ability to continue navigating uncomfortable situations and emotions. When we know that the Holy Spirit is always with us and is our Helper, then there should be no doubt that we can manage our emotions and not allow them to rule us. Knowing that the Holy Spirit is our Helper can be a useful ingredient to add to your thoughts as you practice your being renewed skill. Despite feeling alone, you can remind yourself that you are never alone.

In addition to this revelation, it is essential that we understand God's love for us and continue to grow in our knowledge of that love. The more we understand God's love for us and that his "perfect love casts out fear," the more assurance we have that he is always with us in these situations and that he has not designed us to be ruled by negative emotions.

Practically speaking, this understanding of God's love can be facilitated by meditating on Scriptures that speak to his love, memorizing these Scriptures, using these Scriptures as cues that you can place on important objects in your environment, and strategically using these verses in uncomfortable situations. Remind yourself "to know the love of Christ which passes knowledge; that you may be filled with all the fullness of God" (Ephesians 3:19), and know that "hope does not disappoint, because the love of God has been poured out in our hearts by the Holy Spirit who was given to us" (Romans 5:5). You are loved by God, and we have a supernatural hope from the Holy Spirit that surpasses what we comprehend with our five senses.

As we've discussed, the emotion of fear is in response to real danger at its core. Some of us, however, remain trapped in a cycle of fear because we have learned to tell ourselves that we are in danger when we aren't. The word *fear* comes from the Greek word *phobos*, meaning "flight," or "that which is caused by being scared," but also "that which may cause flight" in response to "fear, dread, or terror."[1] In mental health settings, this is where we get the word *phobia*, which suggests a significant fear that is triggered by the presence of a specific object or situation. In other words, any situation that causes one to be so overwhelmed with intense emotion that they feel the need to escape or avoid the situation is what we mean by *fear*.

Feeling the need to escape with fight or flight can also be triggered by other negative emotional experiences. Shame and guilt can reach a level of distress that triggers the urge to escape a situation if you believe you have not met a particular standard. Intense sadness can also trigger an urge to escape and withdraw from a given situation. Believing that your concept of fairness has been violated may prompt someone to escape a situation in response to anger. Feeling disgusted by perceived or actual contamination can prompt a similar reaction.

As you prepare to be consistent in mastering your emotions, this is the beauty of the words contained in 1 John 4:17-19: because God loves you so much, he has made a way for you to remain strong in situations that trigger intense emotions. The key, however, is allowing yourself to receive his love and know, as it says in Hebrews 13:5, that he will "never leave you nor forsake you."

Also, consider John 8:31-32: "Then Jesus said to those Jews who believed Him, 'If you abide in My word, you are My disciples indeed. And you shall know the truth, and the truth shall make you free.'" It is the truth that we know that makes us free, and we are required to abide, or remain, in the Word to know the truth. Just as being a disciple and remaining in the Word are necessary to be free, reminding yourself of what you've learned in this book and practicing the skills consistently will help you experience freedom over intense emotions. In short, a combination of abiding in the Word of God and continuing to practice the skills you've learned will produce the most victory!

As a result of this manual, you should now understand where the tendency to experience intense emotions began, the adaptive nature of emotions, the importance of understanding triggers, and the consequences of emotional responses. You should also be equipped with several skills to help you navigate emotions, including being present in his presence, being renewed (the new me), being adaptive (engaging in adaptive behaviors), and being physical (tolerating physical sensations). It is now time to put on your full armor and learn how to take all of this wisdom and "get understanding" (Proverbs 4:7).

Let's review what you have learned throughout this journey:

1. Emotions serve an adaptive purpose in your life; they are meant to help you navigate your world and are not meant to harm you.

2. A tendency toward intense emotionality began in the Garden of Eden, and this tendency, known as *neuroticism*, set the stage for many of us to view negative emotions as dangerous. This tendency is both genetic and environmental but can be reprogrammed.

3. The ways we have learned to respond to certain emotions is the issue, not the emotion itself.

4. You can "be transformed by the renewing of your mind" (Romans 12:2) and learn to master emotions.

5. The "being" skills (being present, being renewed, being adaptive, and being physical) are all supported by Scripture and all require being "doers" and "not hearers only" (James 1:22).

6. The skills taught throughout this book require regular practice.

BEING CONSISTENT: THE IMPORTANCE OF PRACTICE

Learning to view emotions as dangerous and developing the belief that you can't handle certain emotions happened over a period of time. As you can imagine, learning any new skill requires practice and consistency. You have been equipped with evidence-based skills that are founded on the truth of God's Word, and you have been given a blueprint for success. What does success look like? It may be when you and others have observed that you have broken patterns of avoidance, or that you are not responding to emotional triggers in a dysregulated fashion (e.g., wrath, isolation, shutting down). It may be when you have been able to enjoy pleasurable activities more than you used to, or you have been able to remain present during a task where you have historically been distracted. It may be when your awareness of emotional intensity occurs before your response, or when you are more productive at home or work, or when you are engaging in healthy habits that were not previously a part of your routine (e.g., regular exercise, healthy eating).

It is important that you extend grace to yourself and normalize emotions such as frustration and disappointment if changes are not occurring as fast as you would like. Many of these emotional patterns began in childhood and they take time to reprogram. However, with consistency and trust in the Lord, your victory is an adaptive response away.

Though this manual was developed for both individuals and groups, I encourage you to enlist the help of someone that you do life with (preferably someone who is familiar with this book). As noted in Hebrews 10:25, we are not to forsake "the assembling of ourselves together, as *is* the manner of some." As members of the body of Christ, we are stronger when all the parts of the body are joined and functioning well together. Therefore, as you create your Being Consistent plan, identify someone who may hold you accountable while speaking encouraging words. Along these lines, remember the following principles as you learn the importance of being consistent.

1. ***Practice regularly.*** Just like the gospel message is simple to understand but often not easy to practice, understanding how to use these skills on a regular basis is simple to understand but not easy to practice. It is simple in the sense that you will have plenty of opportunities to have your emotions triggered, which allows you to practice your skills. It is not easy in the sense that this process will be uncomfortable. As I have emphasized throughout this book, however, you are fully equipped to tolerate intense emotions, to "ride the wave" of discomfort, and to master your emotions. Setting aside time to practice each week will guarantee your success over time. You will not be perfect in your practice, but remember who dwells on the inside of you is perfect, and you are in the process of being transformed into his image on the outside.

2. ***Activate the Patient Soul skill.*** As we've mentioned throughout this manual, the way you respond to emotions is a learned

behavior. Unlearning the ways you respond to emotions requires you to replace your usual responses with new responses that allow you to pay attention to your emotions and not judge them as they are occurring. The Patient Soul (PS) skill will be helpful in *any* situation that you encounter, but you must develop a plan to practice it. One hack to use when you are in an uncomfortable situation is to memorize the second component of the PS skill.

3. ***Remember your emotional triad.*** As a reminder, the second component of the PS skill involves remembering your emotional triad:

- What am I thinking in this moment?
- What am I feeling in my body in this moment?
- What am I doing / do I feel like doing in this moment?

4. ***Use the Being Consistent worksheet for accountability.*** The worksheets found throughout this manual are specifically designed to provide you with a sense of mastery and control while keeping you accountable. The Being Consistent worksheet (at the end of this chapter) will assist you with maintaining your skills long term and it will give you something to refer to in the future. This worksheet also allows you to provide details about how you will be held accountable with your new skills and be an encourager for someone else in your life.

REFLECTION: BEING CONSISTENT

If you are completing the Being Consistent worksheet (at the end of this chapter) in a group, please take this time to go over the details with your group members. This is a perfect opportunity to discuss how you will regularly use your new skills of "being." Ask for feedback from those you trust, about discomfort ratings, avoidance ratings, items that you may need for your being brave exposures, and creative ways to confront intense emotions. Also, take this time to identify someone to help you with accountability in completing your list of uncomfortable situations, preferably someone who is familiar with this book. As already mentioned, having weekly in-person meetings, text messages, and phone calls will enhance your understanding of emotions and improve your relationships, since "iron sharpens iron" (Proverbs 27:17).

Take a look at your Being Consistent worksheet. Look at the four "being" skills and answer the following questions, either during your alone time or within your life group.

1. What is your main takeaway from "Being Present"? How will this skill help you in different areas of your life?

2. What is your main takeaway from "Being Renewed"? How will this skill help you in different areas of your life?

3. What is your main takeaway from "Being Adaptive"? How will this skill help you in different areas of your life?

4. What is your main takeaway from "Being Physical"? How will this skill help you in different areas of your life?

5. What is your favorite thing that you learned throughout this book? How do you see this impacting your life?

6. *Read* 1 John 4:17-19. What does this Scripture mean to you as you continue navigating situations that trigger a range of emotions?

7. *Read* Deuteronomy 31:6; Joshua 1:5; Psalm 71:1; and Hebrews 13:5. What do these Scriptures mean to you as you continue your journey of navigating situations that may trigger intense emotions?

SUMMARY

There are a number of Scriptures that were hand-selected for you throughout your journey with this manual, and as we conclude our journey together, I want to remind you of several of them. First John 4:17 reminds us that "as He is, so are we in this world." Romans 5:3-4 tells us that we are to glory in tribulation, "knowing that tribulation produces perseverance; and perseverance, character; and character, hope." Hebrews 4:15 states, "For we do not have a High Priest who cannot sympathize with our weaknesses, but was in all *points* tempted as *we are, yet* without sin."

Each of these passages can apply to the new skills you have learned. Let me give you a word of encouragement based on the Scriptures above. First, we have power and authority through Jesus to navigate any situation. Second, as believers, we have the ability to approach trials and tribulations differently. We have an assurance of victory because of what is produced on the inside of us as we navigate tribulation. Finally, Jesus "gets it" and experienced the same emotions that we do on a regular basis and did so successfully! Despite what we've learned to think, what experiences we may have had, and the devastating situations we may have overcome, we *are* more than conquerors and designed to master our emotions. As you take hold of this revelation, God will begin to open doors so that you can share this good news and disciple those around you. Amen.

THE BEING CONSISTENT WORKSHEET

This worksheet should be used in holding yourself accountable so that you can maintain consistency in managing emotions.

What are some situations in your life where practicing this skill will be important?

How will you be held accountable to this skill?

BEING PRESENT

BEING PRESENT

BEING RENEWED

BEING RENEWED

BEING ADAPTIVE

BEING ADAPTIVE

BEING PHYSICAL

BEING PHYSICAL

ACKNOWLEDGMENTS

To Jackie, Jada, and Mya, the loves of my life. I continue to write with you in mind like I'm running out of time. Words cannot adequately express my love for you. May I continue to honor you always.

To my mother, Harriett. Your early sacrifices planted significant seeds. Cheers to the harvest.

To my colleagues at InterVarsity Press. Thank you for your feedback and support throughout this process. Your love for the Lord has been palpable and your encouragement toward me has fueled the fire.

To my church family at CLC. Thank you for your love and support.

To my friends and colleagues at KYCARDS, I love and appreciate you. Continue fighting the good fight.

To my many psychology mentors and friends. I remain eternally grateful for your imparting of scientific knowledge and wisdom. My training continues to serve a greater purpose. CBT works.

To AWMI and Charis Bible College. The revelation I have received from your teachings is indescribable. May this manual provide an additional resource, particularly for those whose "battle is between their ears."

To the body of Christ. I trust that this manual will add arrows to your quiver. Be strong and courageous, because that is who you really are.

Finally, to negative emotions. I see you, I understand you, I respect you, and I value you. However, I refuse to allow the body of Christ to be dominated by you.

NOTES

1. IN THE BEGINNING

[1]Shannon Sauer-Zavala and David Barlow, *Neuroticism: A New Framework for Emotional Disorders and Their Treatment* (New York: The Guilford Press, 2021), 23.

2. BEING AN EMOTIONAL MASTER: THE PURPOSE OF YOUR EMOTIONS

[1]David Barlow, *Anxiety and Its Disorders: The Nature and Treatment of Anxiety and Panic* (New York: The Guilford Press, 2002), 105-38.

[2]Barlow, *Anxiety and Its Disorders*, 105-38.

3. BEING AN EMOTIONAL MASTER: THE PARTS OF YOUR EMOTIONS

[1]David Barlow, *Unified Protocol for Transdiagnostic Treatment of Emotional Disorders* (New York: Oxford University Press, 2011), 13-15.

[2]Michelle Craske et al., "Maximizing Exposure Therapy: An Inhibitory Learning Approach," *Behaviour Research and Therapy* 58 (2014): 10-23.

[3]Rochelle Frank and Joan Davidson, *The Transdiagnostic Road Map to Case Formulation and Treatment Planning* (Oakland, CA: New Harbinger Publications Inc., 2014), 24.

[4]Kevin Chapman and Janet Woodruff-Borden, "The Impact of Family Functioning on Anxiety Symptoms in African American and European American Young Adults," *Personality and Individual Differences* 47 (2009): 583-89; and Kevin Chapman, Jenny Petrie, Lauren Vines, and Janet Woodruff-Borden, "The Co-occurrence of Anxiety Disorders Among African American Parents and Their Children," *Journal of Anxiety* 26 (2012): 65-70.

5. BEING PRESENT

[1]Craske et al., "Maximizing Exposure Therapy," 10-23.

6. BEING RENEWED

[1]Michelle Craske et al., *Positive Affect Treatment for Depression and Anxiety* (New York: Oxford University Press, 2022), 56-64.

[2]Judith Beck, *Cognitive Behavior Therapy: Basics and Beyond* (New York: The Guilford Press, 2020), 30-70.

[3]Michelle Craske et al., "Maximizing Exposure Therapy," 10-23.

[4]Marco Catani, Flavio Dell'acqua, and Michel Thiebaut de Schotten, "A Revised Limbic System Model for Memory, Emotion, and Behaviour," *Neuroscience and Biobehavioral Reviews* 37, no. 8 (2013): 1724-37.

7. BEING ADAPTIVE

[1]Aaron Beck, *Cognitive Therapy: Basics and Beyond* (New York: The Guilford Press, 1995); and Jesse Wright et al., *Learning Cognitive-Behavior Therapy: An Illustrated Guide* (Arlington, VA: American Psychiatric Association Publishing, 2017), 6-23.

[2]Craske et al., *Positive Affect Treatment for Depression and Anxiety*, 25-26.

[3]Barlow, *Anxiety and Its Disorder*, 105-38.

[4]Kevin Chapman, Sarah Kurtz, and Janet Woodruff-Borden, "A Structural Equation Model Analysis of Perceived Control and Psychological Distress on Worry Among African American and European American Young Adults," *Journal of Anxiety Disorders* 23 (2009): 69-76; and Frank and Davidson, *The Transdiagnostic Road Map*, 44-45.

[5]Craske et al., "Maximizing Exposure Therapy," 10-23.

8. BEING PHYSICAL

[1]Barlow, *Anxiety and Its Disorders*, 3.

[2]Willem Kop et al., "Autonomic Nervous System Reactivity to Positive and Negative Mood Induction: The Role of Acute Psychological Responses and Frontal Electrocortical Activity," *Biological Psychology* 86, no. 3 (2011): 230-38.

[3]Michael Telch, "The Nature and Causes of Anxiety and Panic," 2015, 1-11, https://labs.la.utexas.edu/telch/files/2015/08/Nature-and-Causes-8.10.15.pdf.

[4]Telch, "The Nature and Causes of Anxiety and Panic," 1-11.

10. BEING CONSISTENT

[1]W. E. Vine, *Vine's Concise Dictionary of the Bible* (Nashville, TN: Thomas Nelson, 2005), 133.